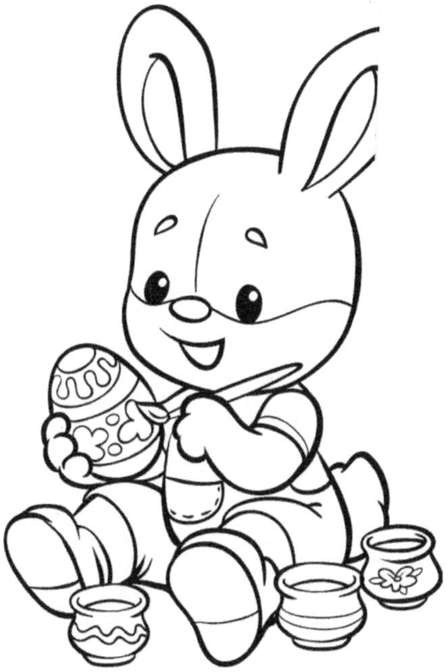

Happy Easter

Coloring Book for Toddlers

CREATIVE COLORING PRESS

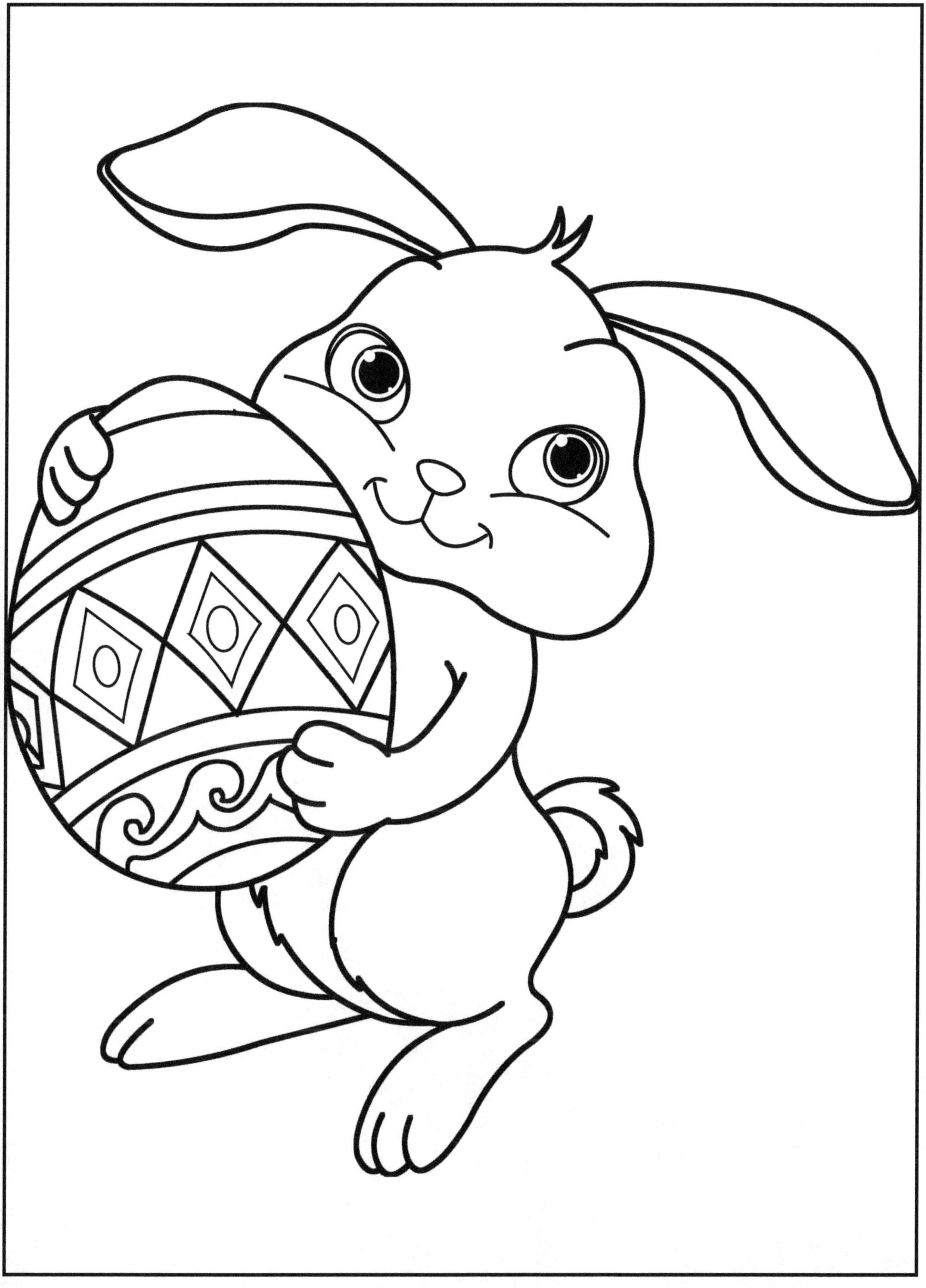

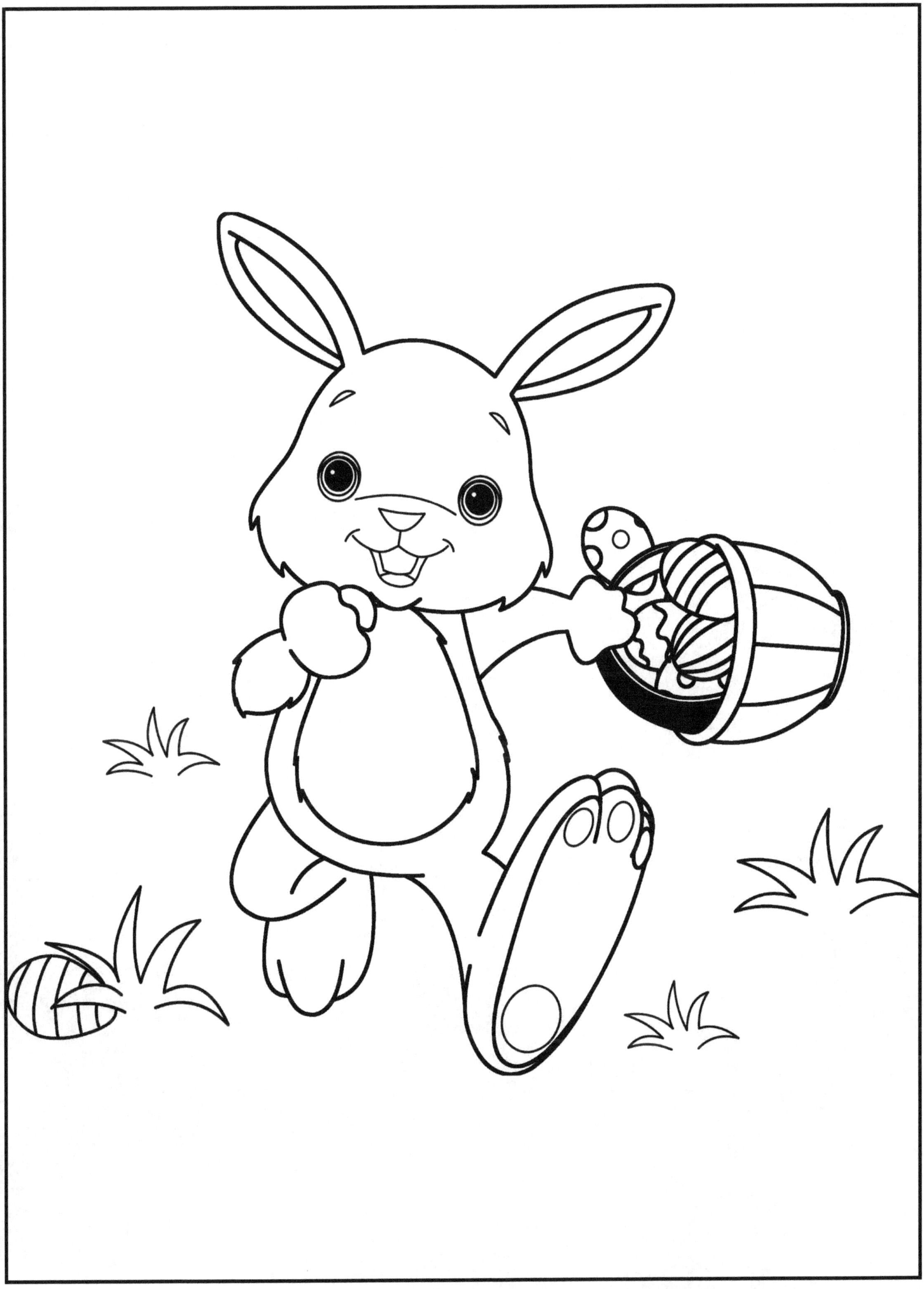

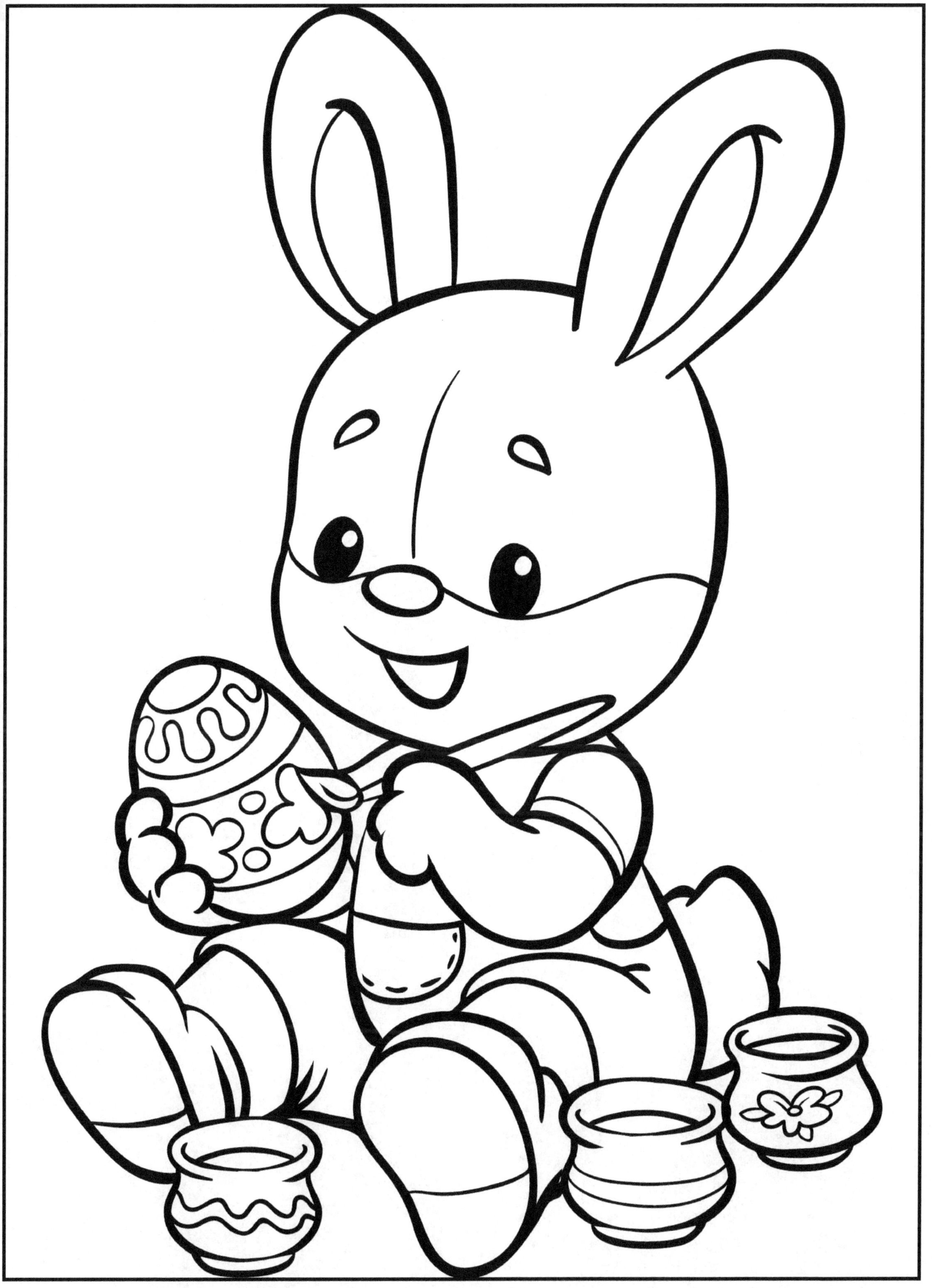

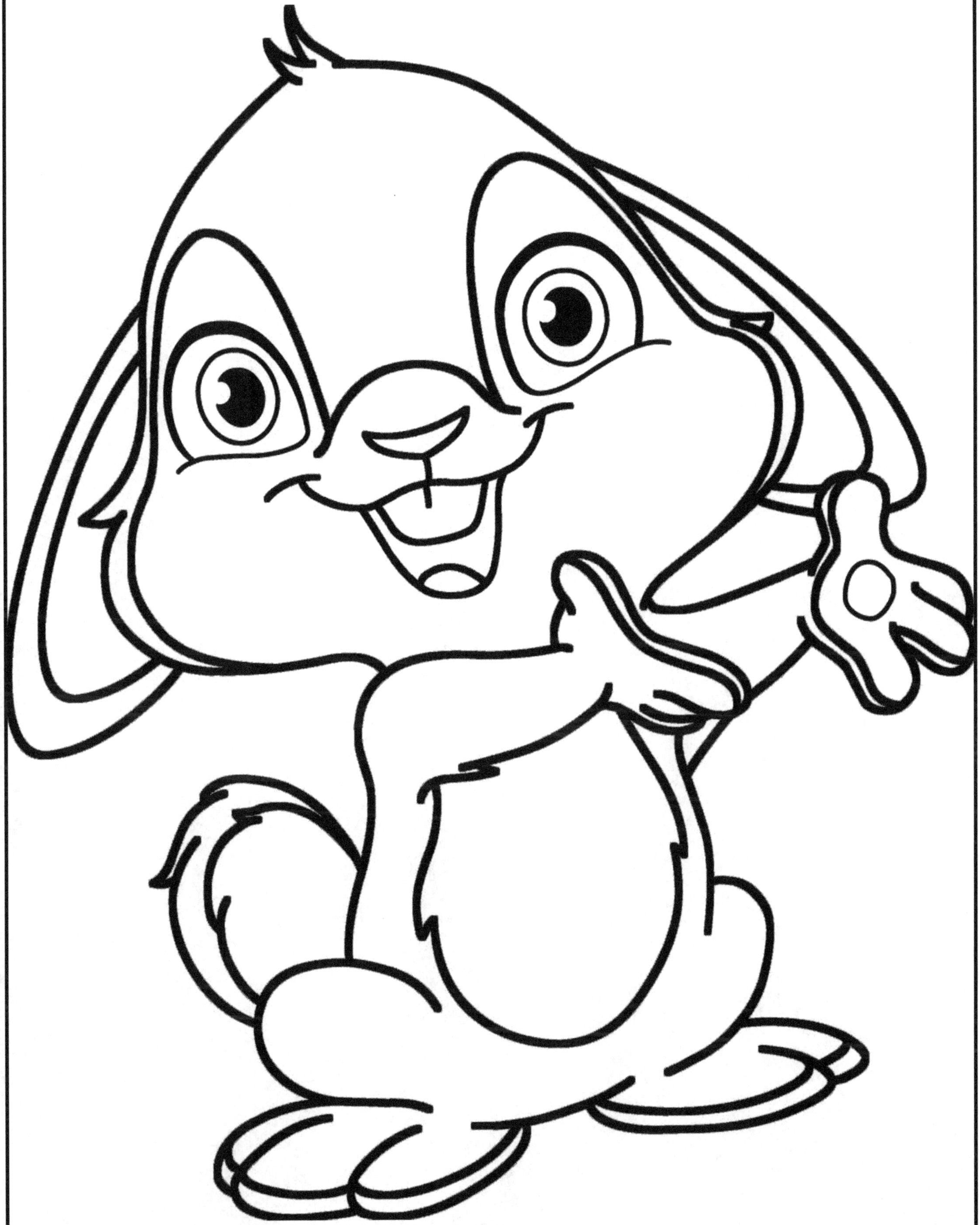

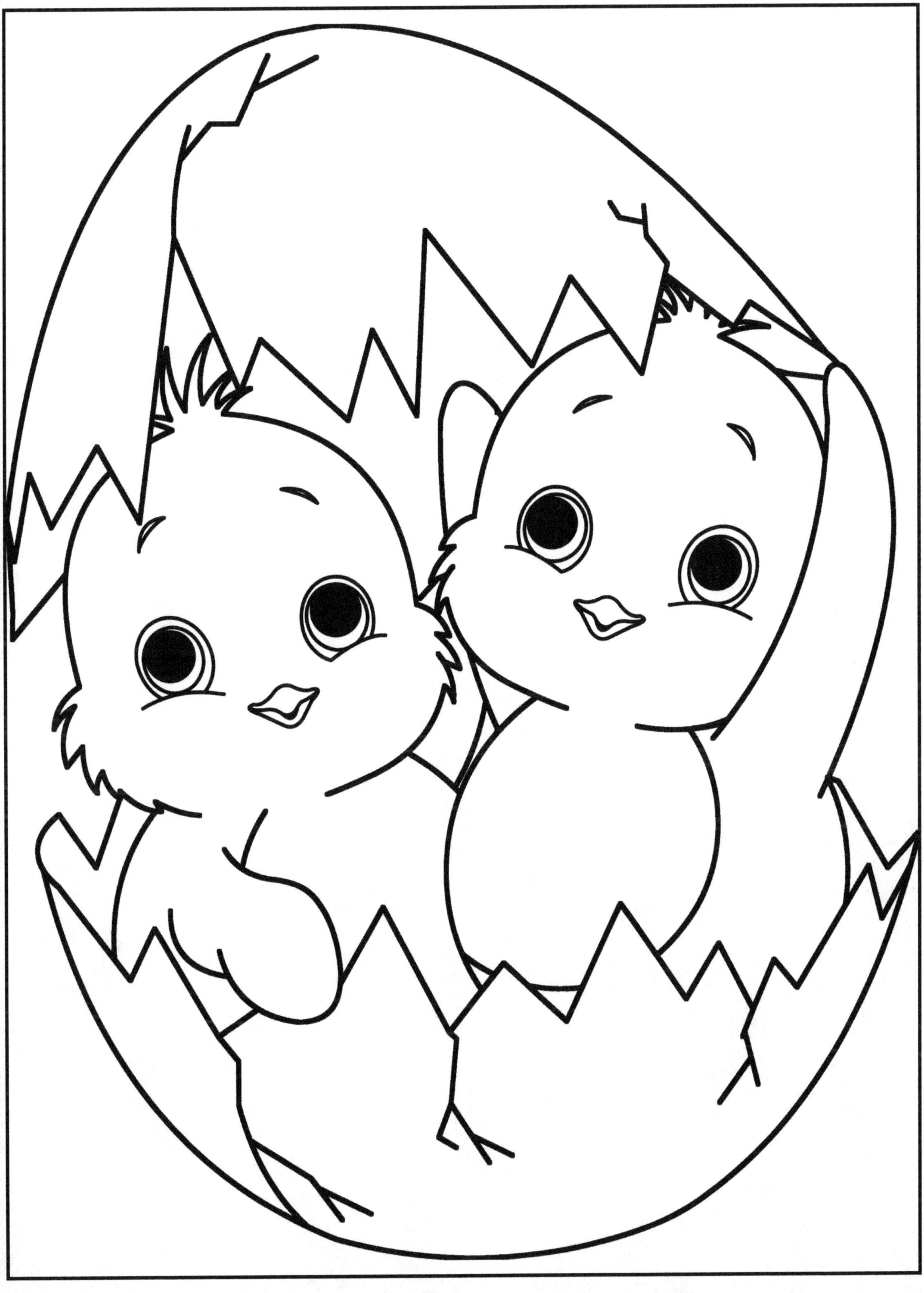

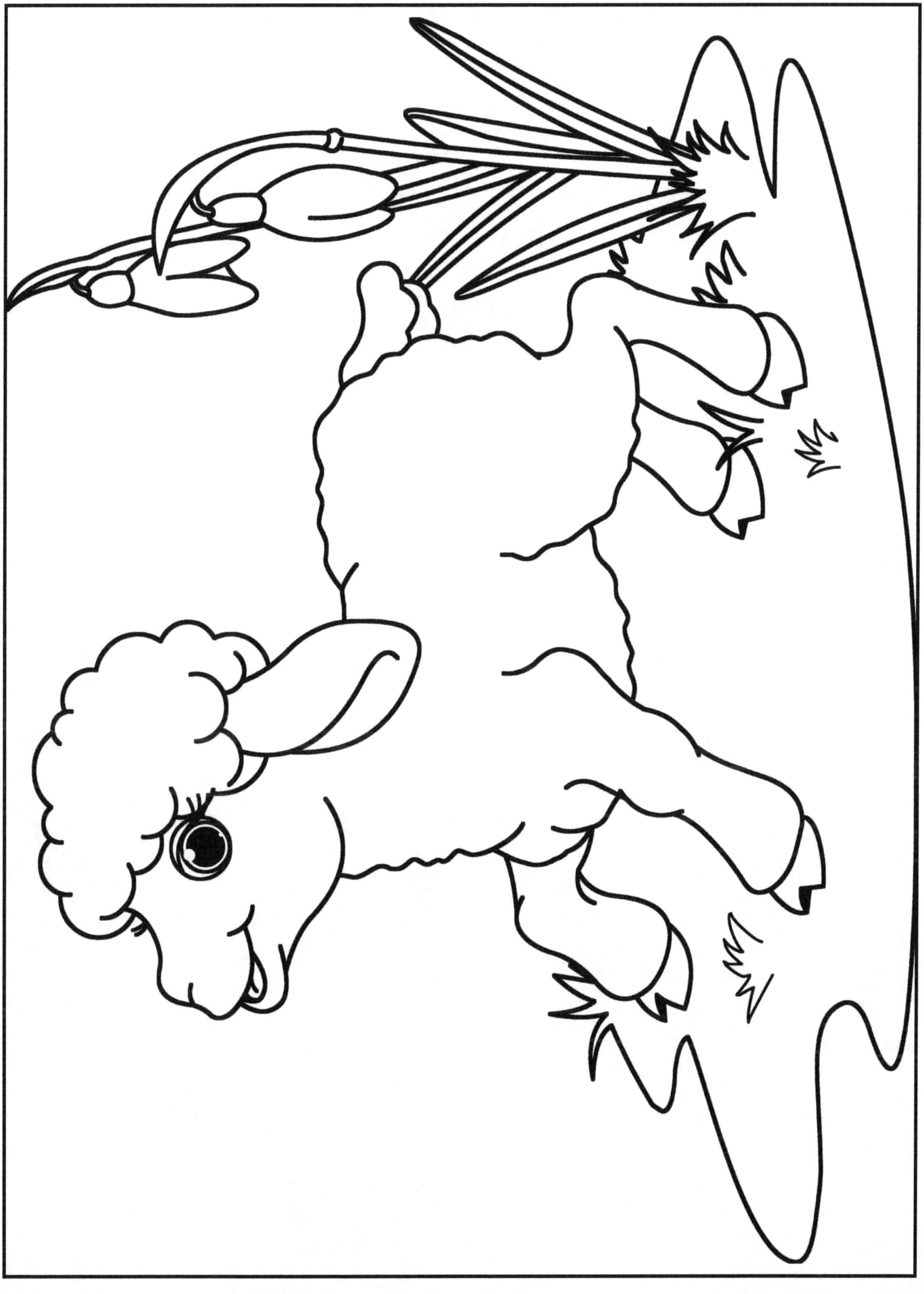

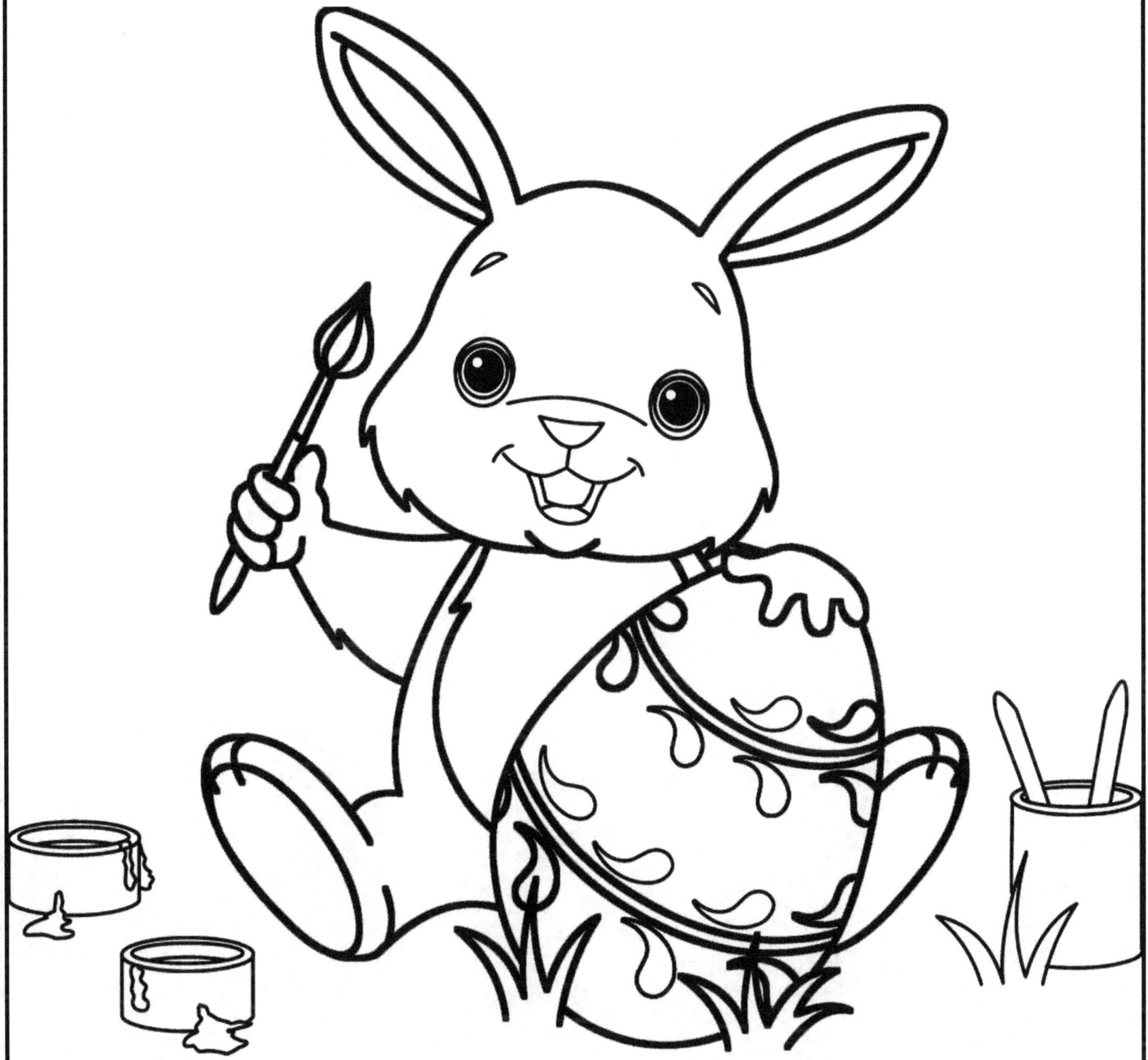

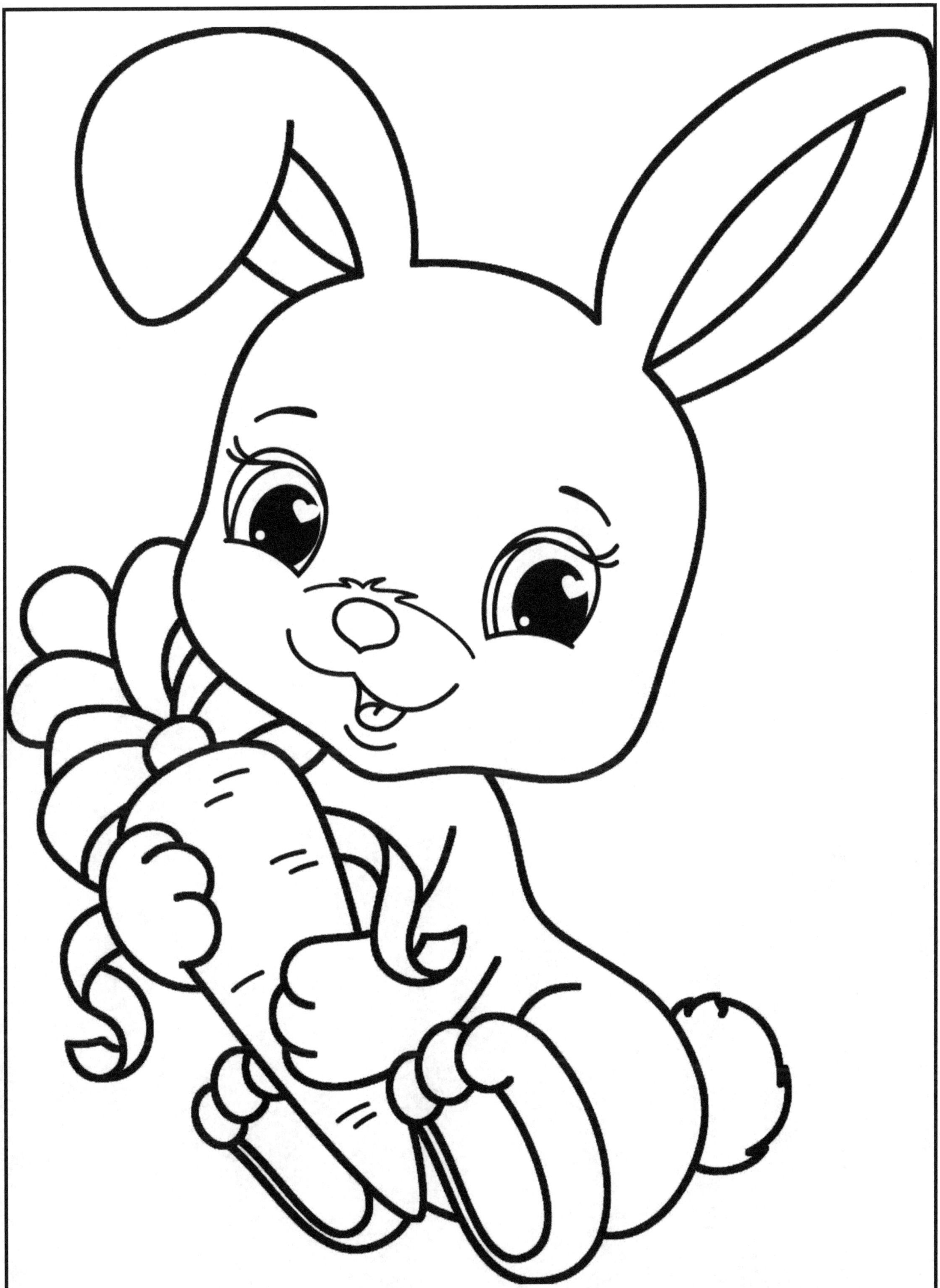

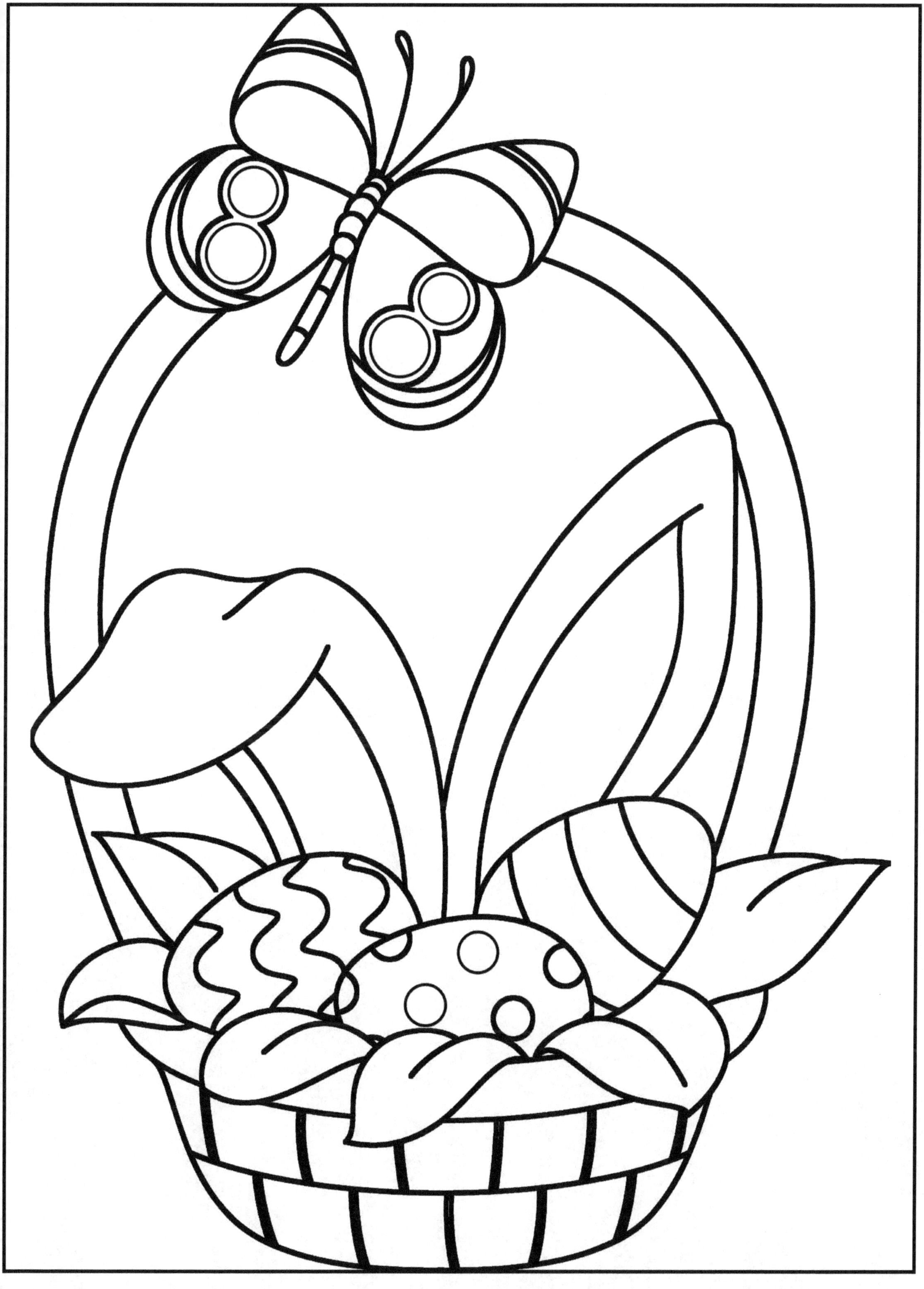

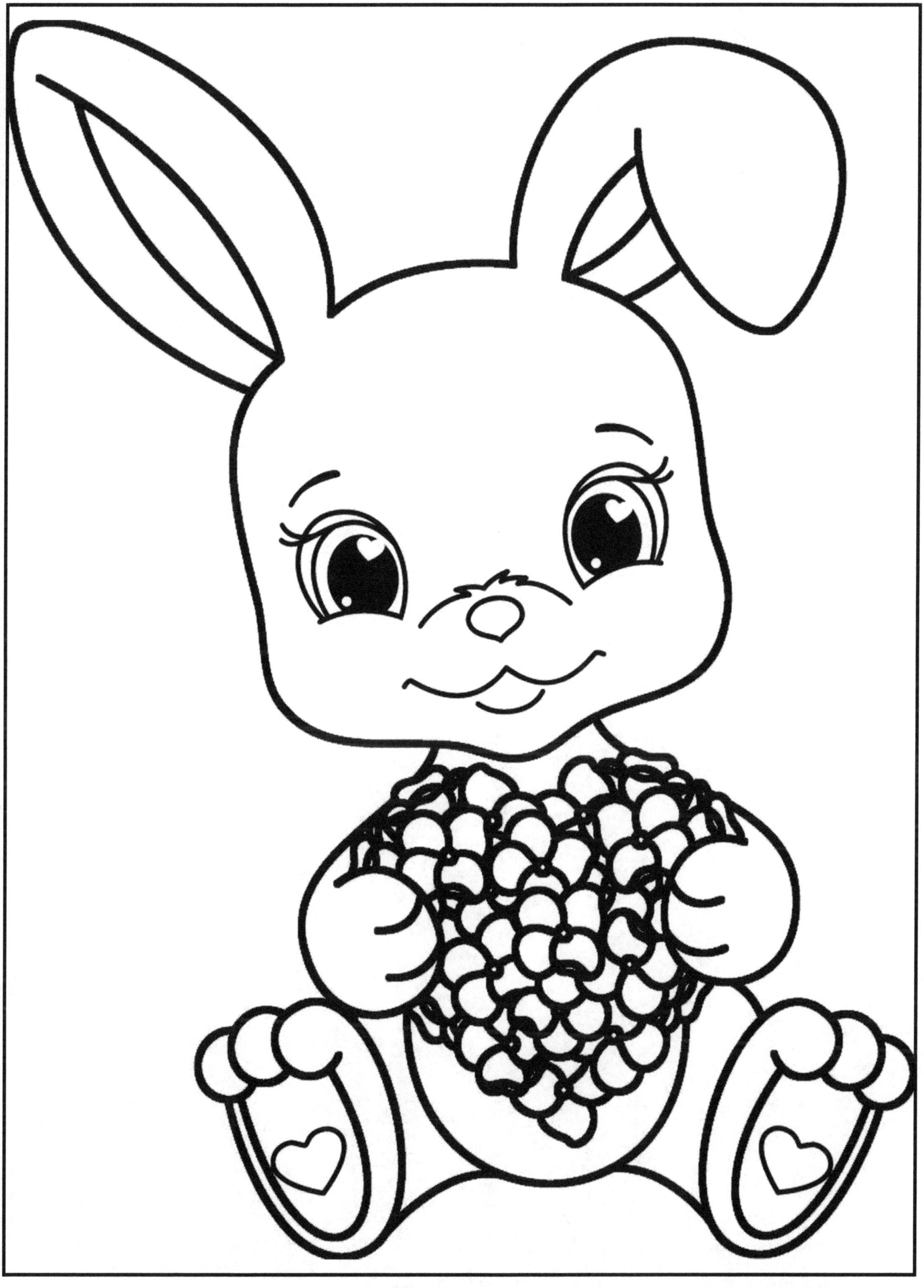

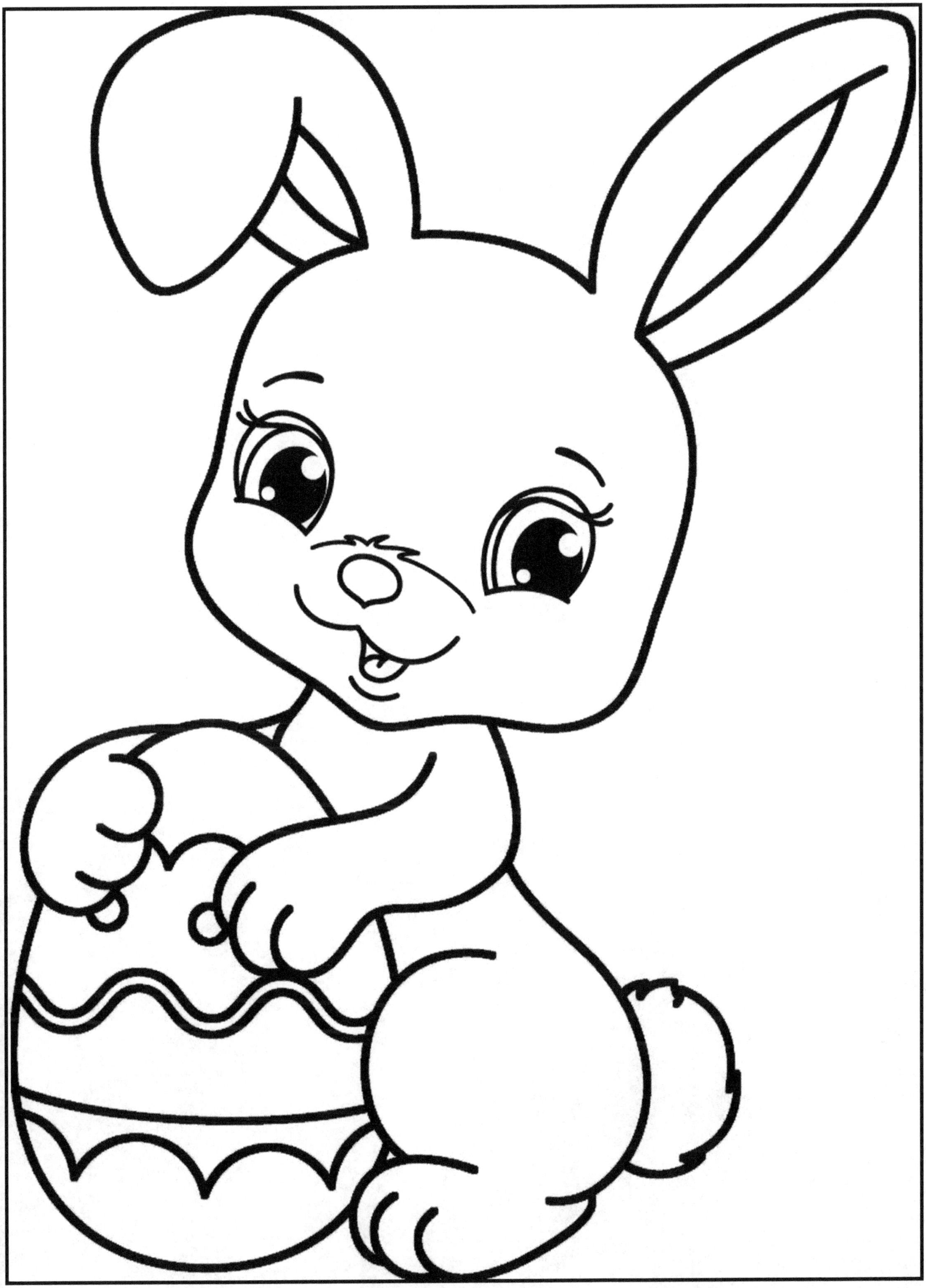

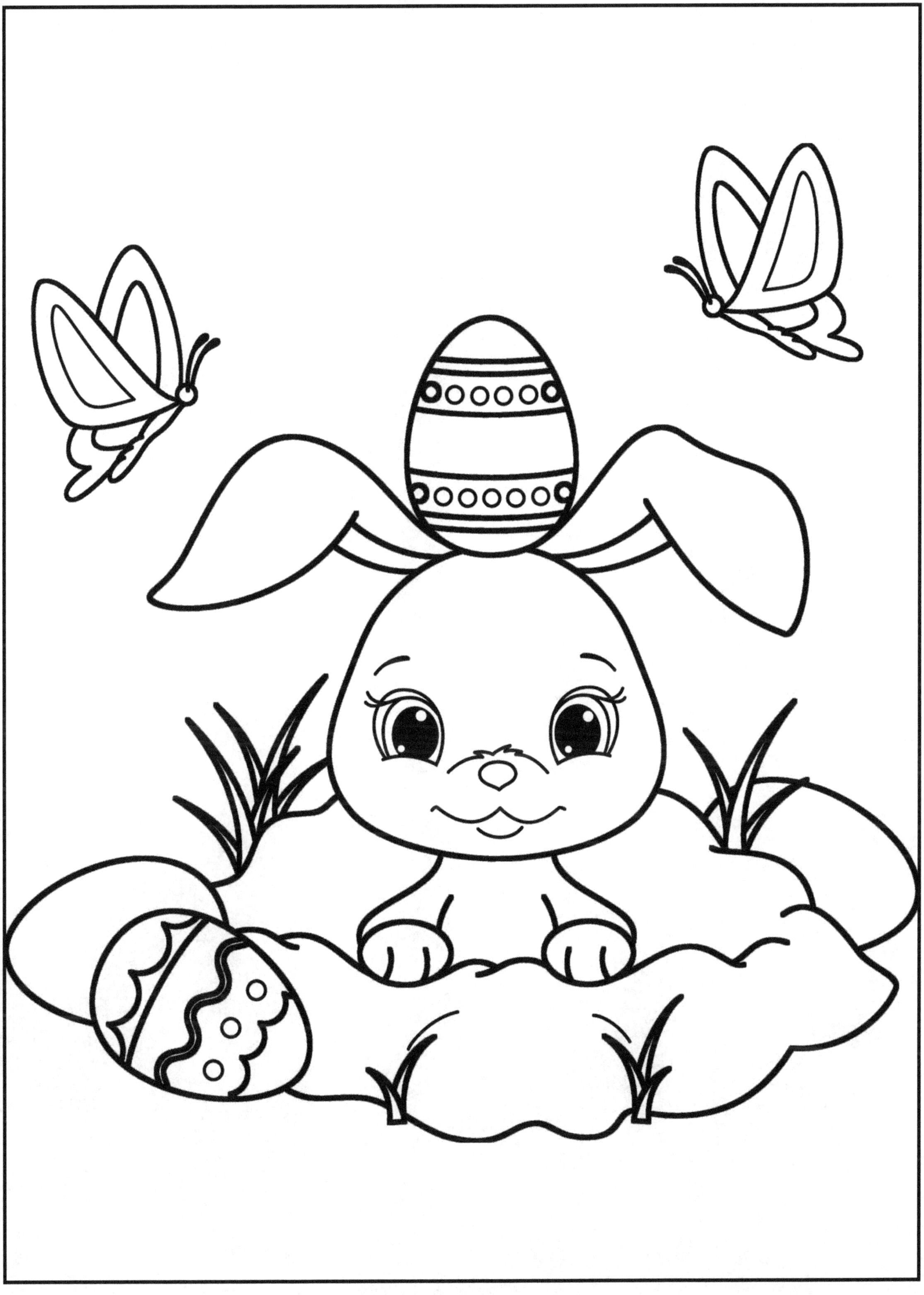

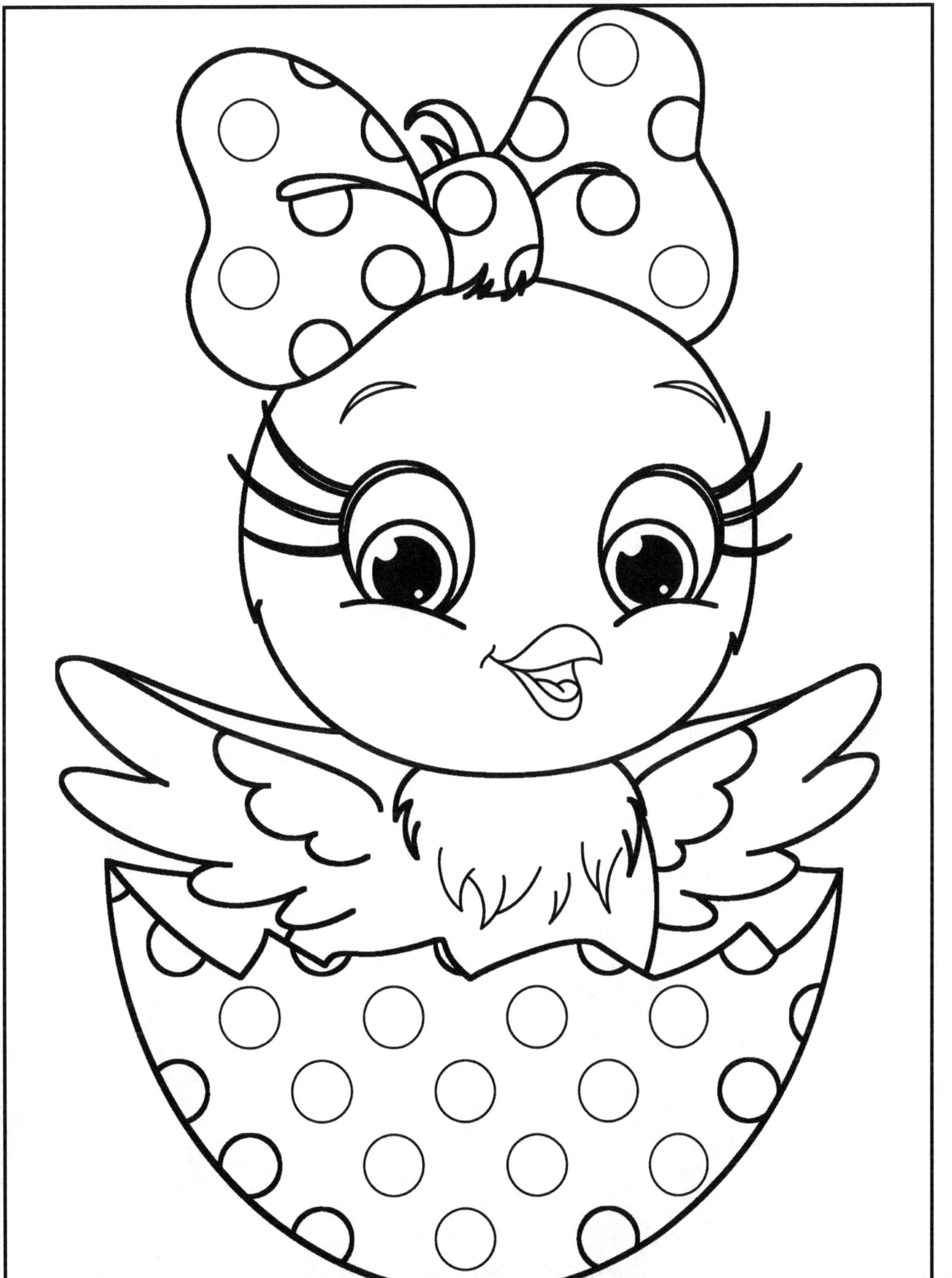

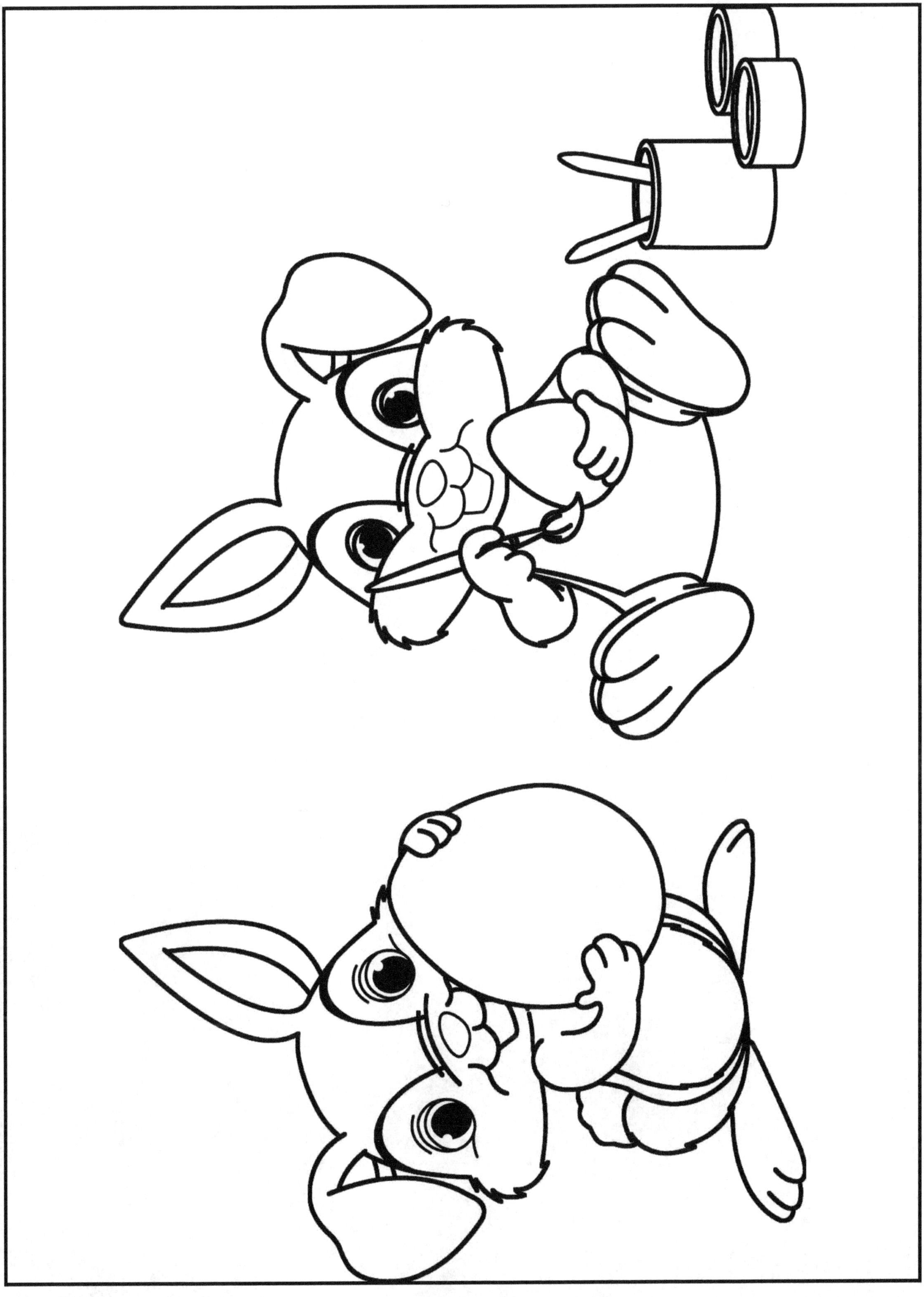

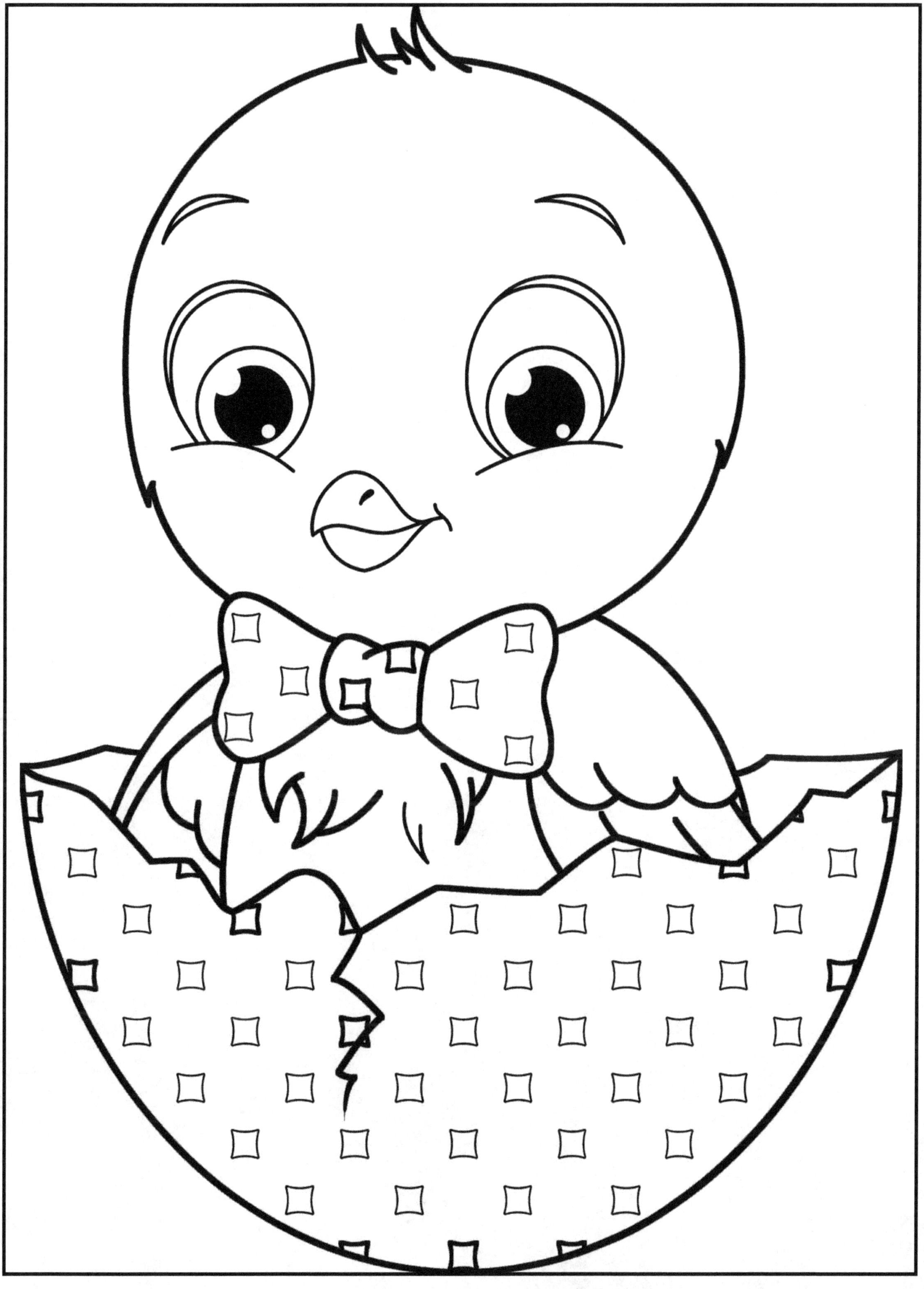

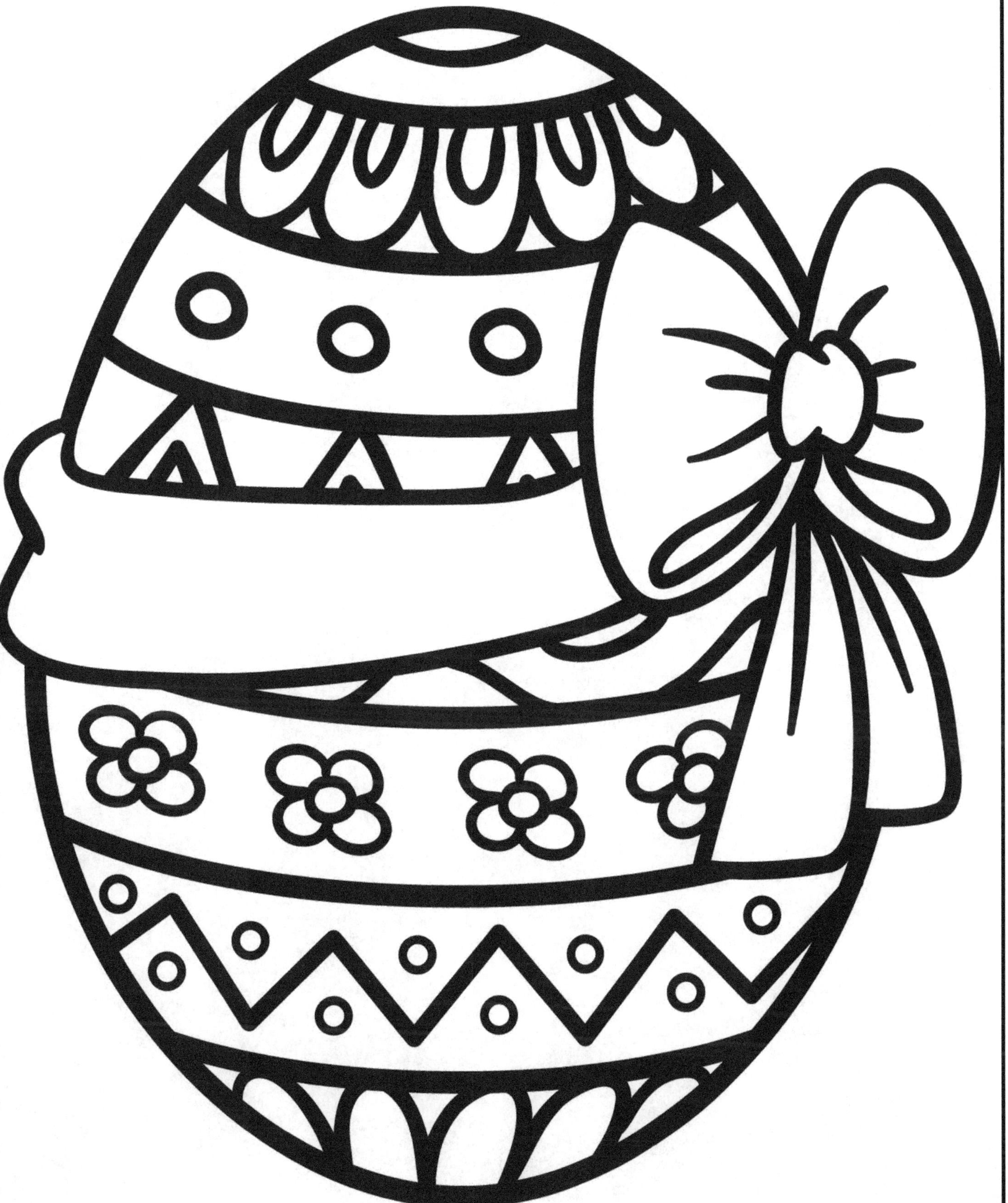

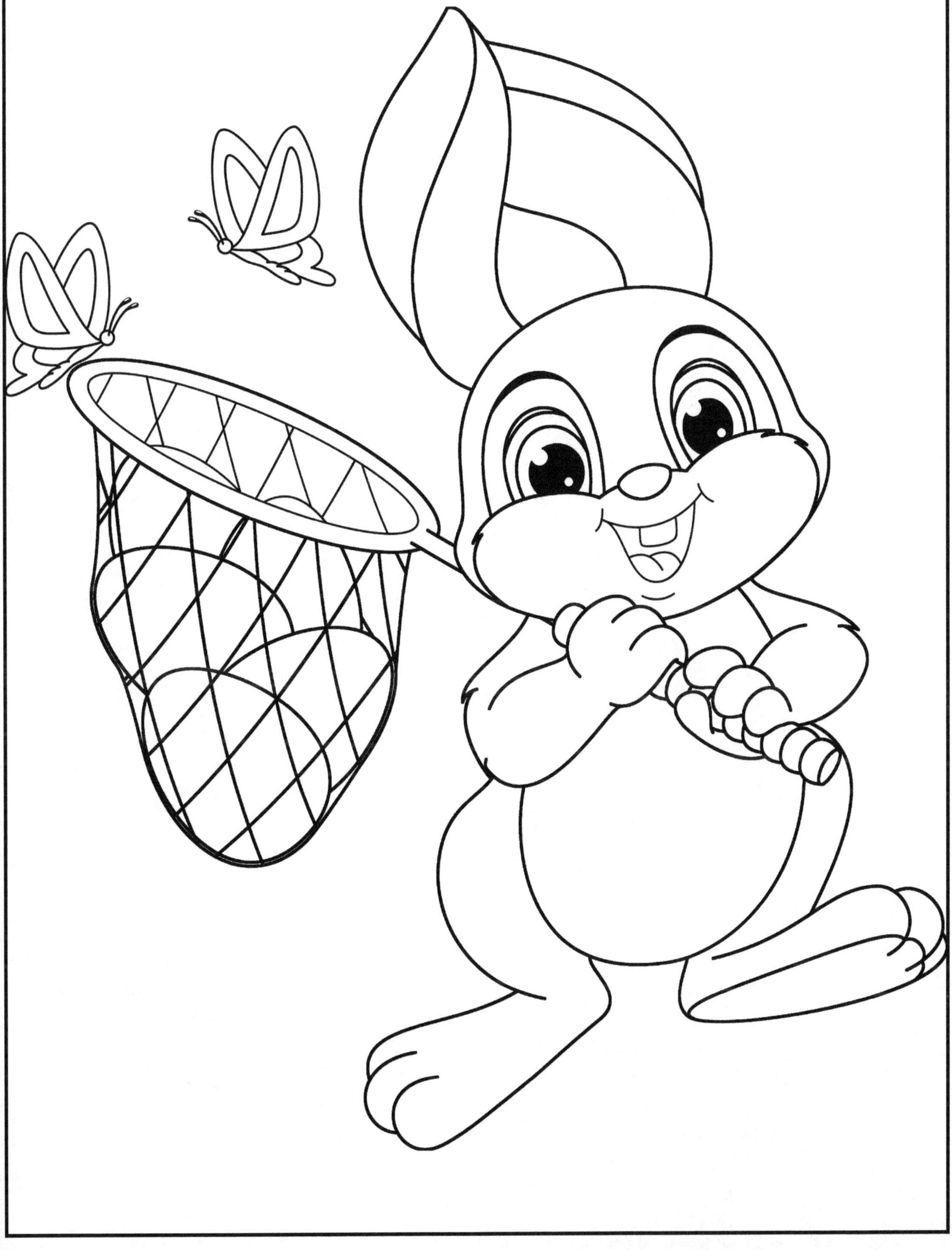

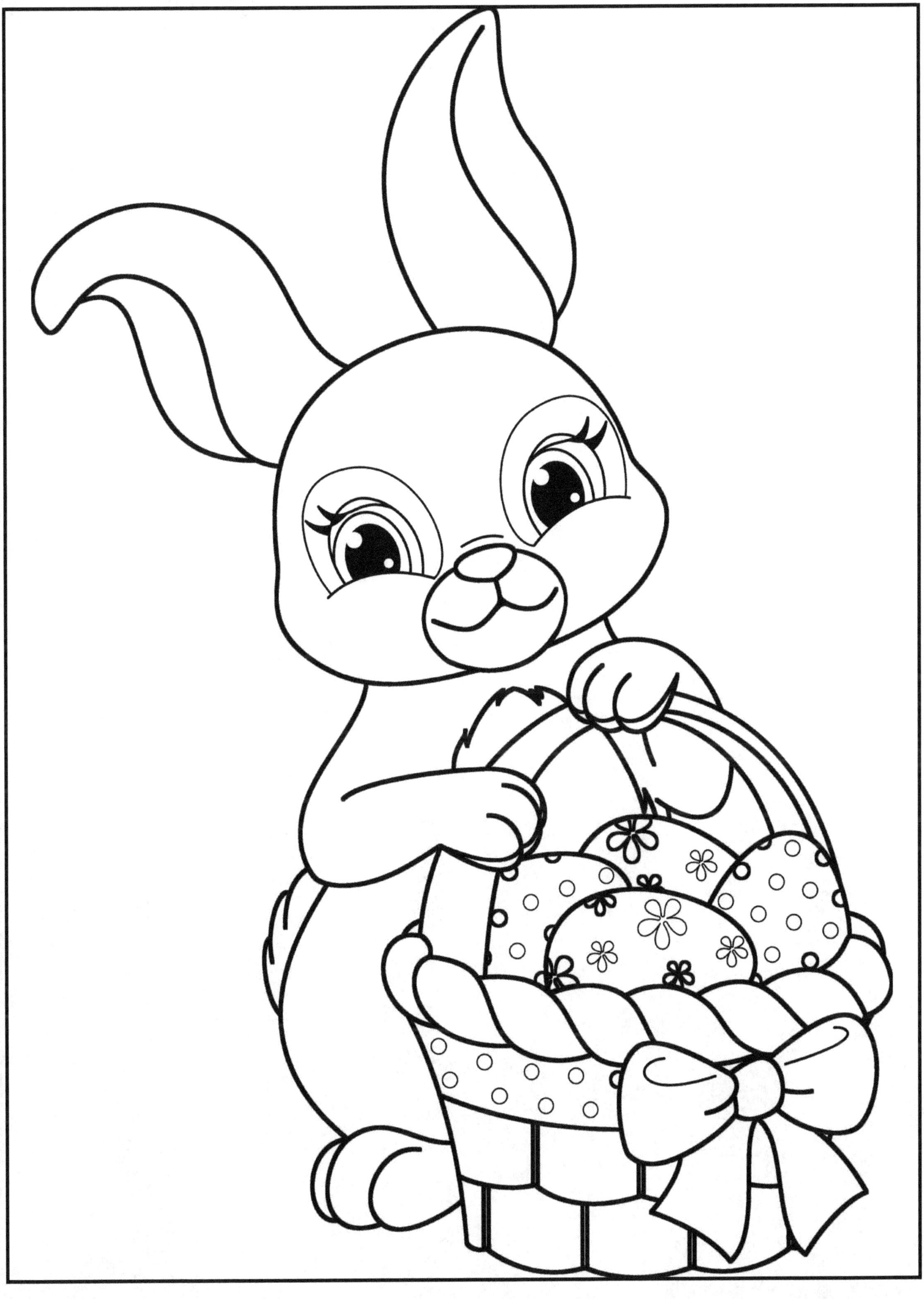

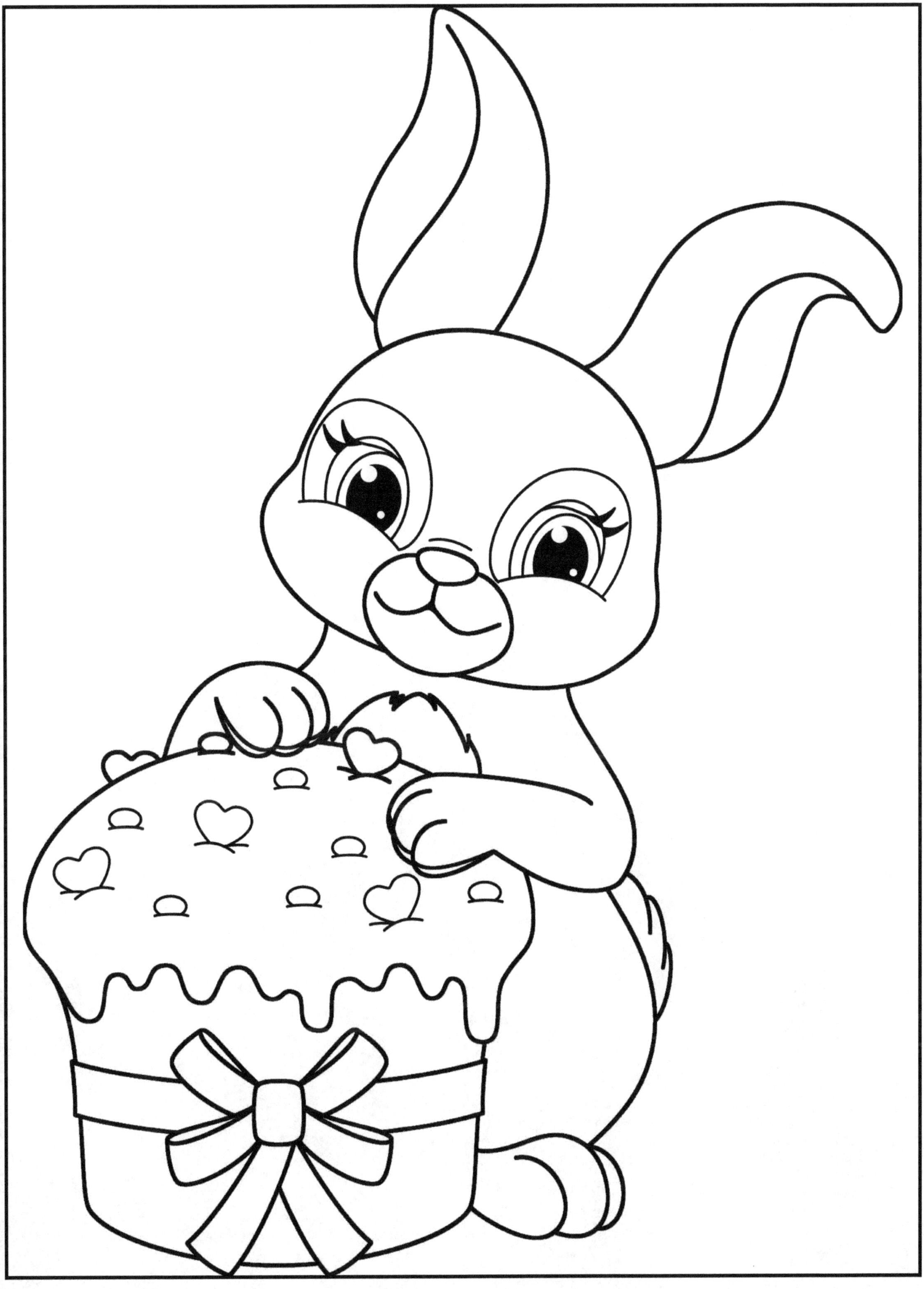

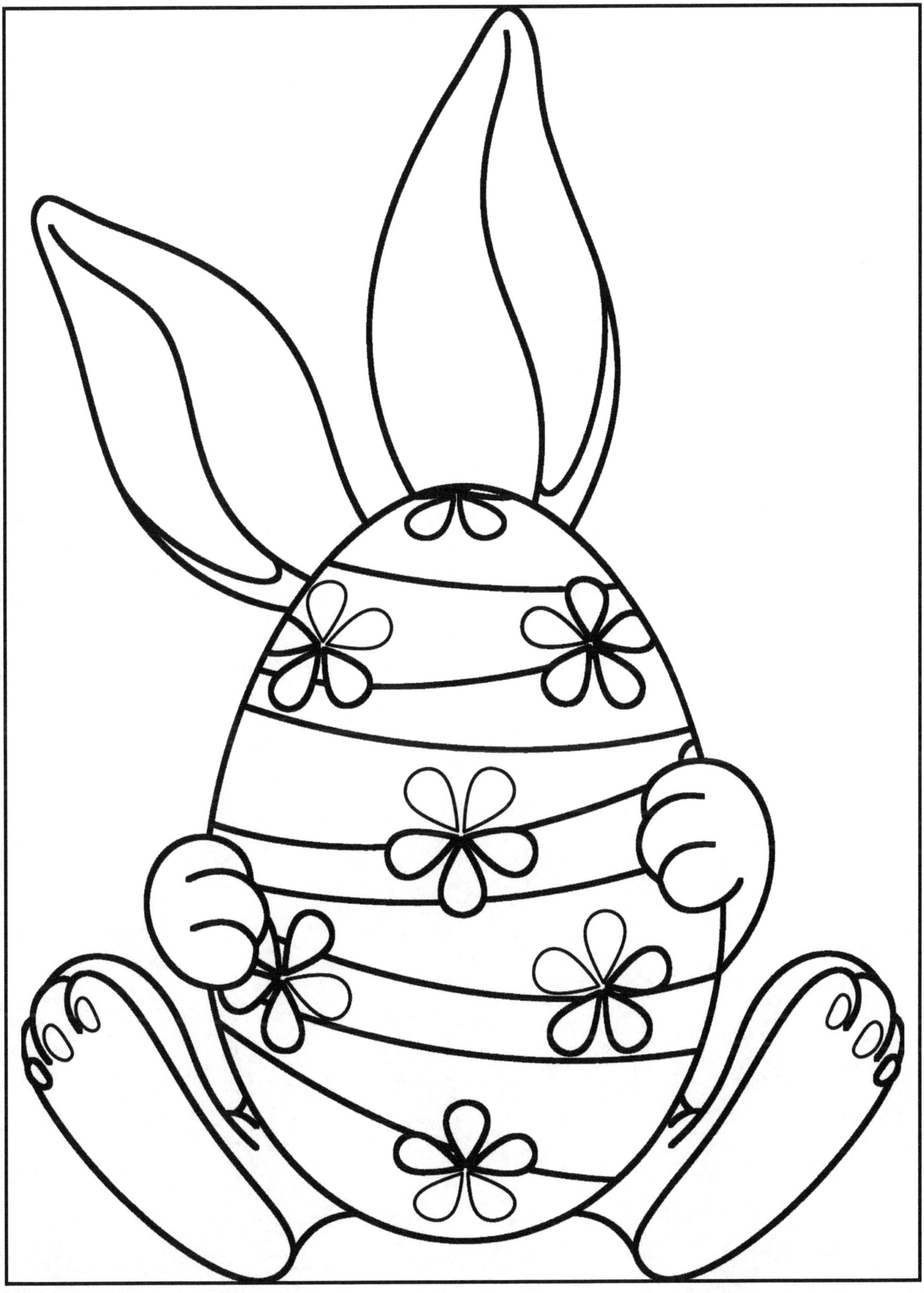

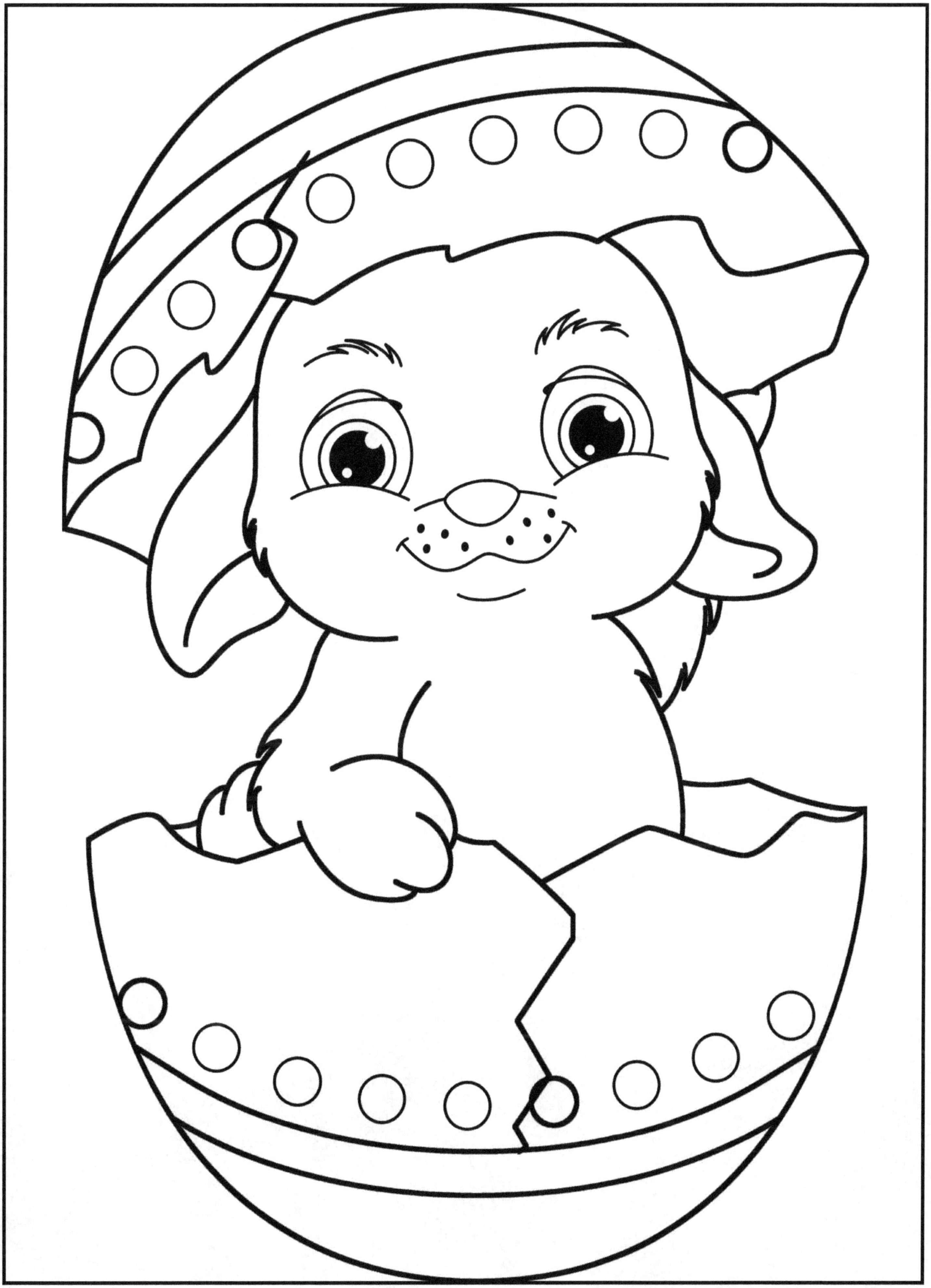

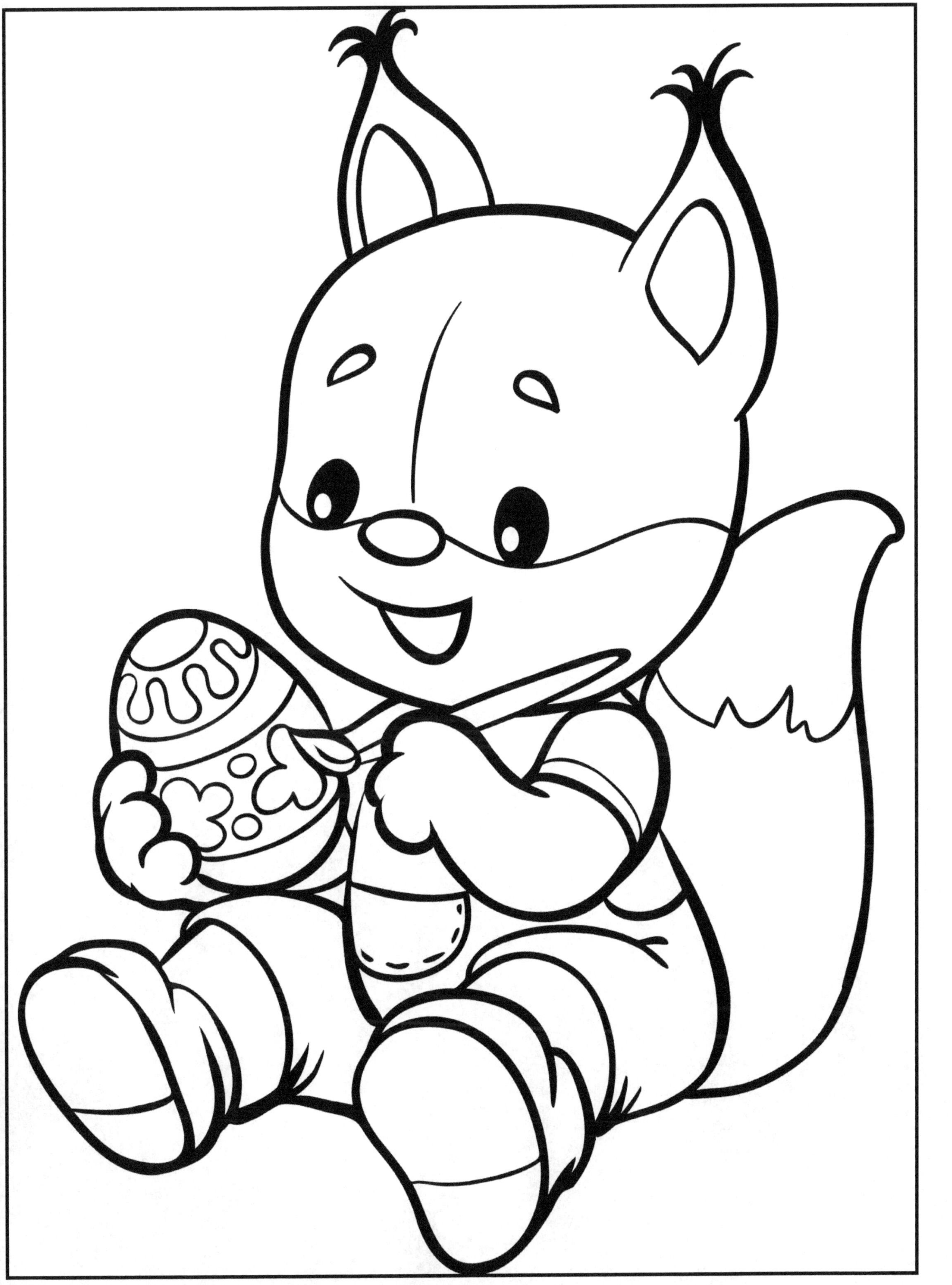

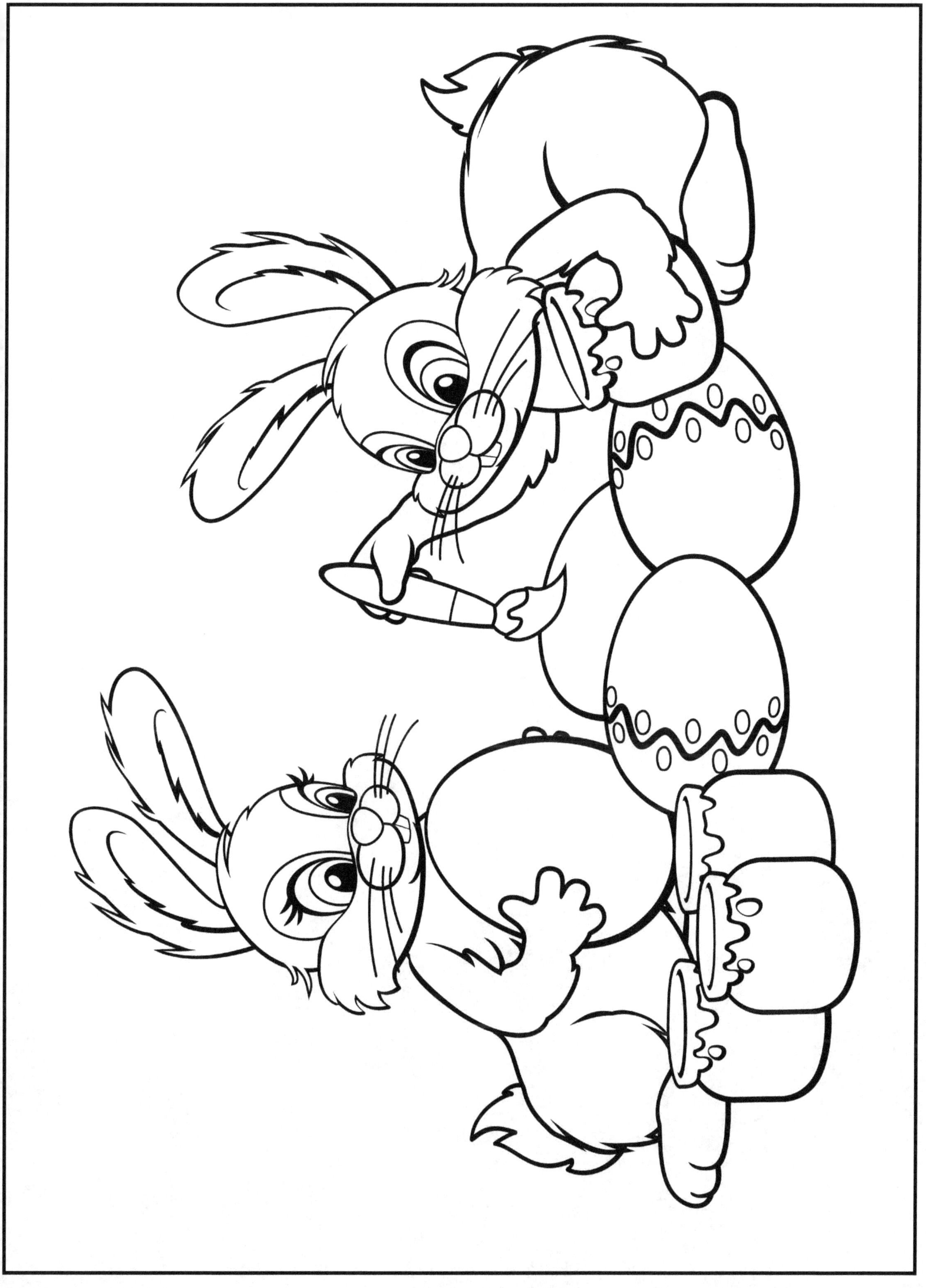

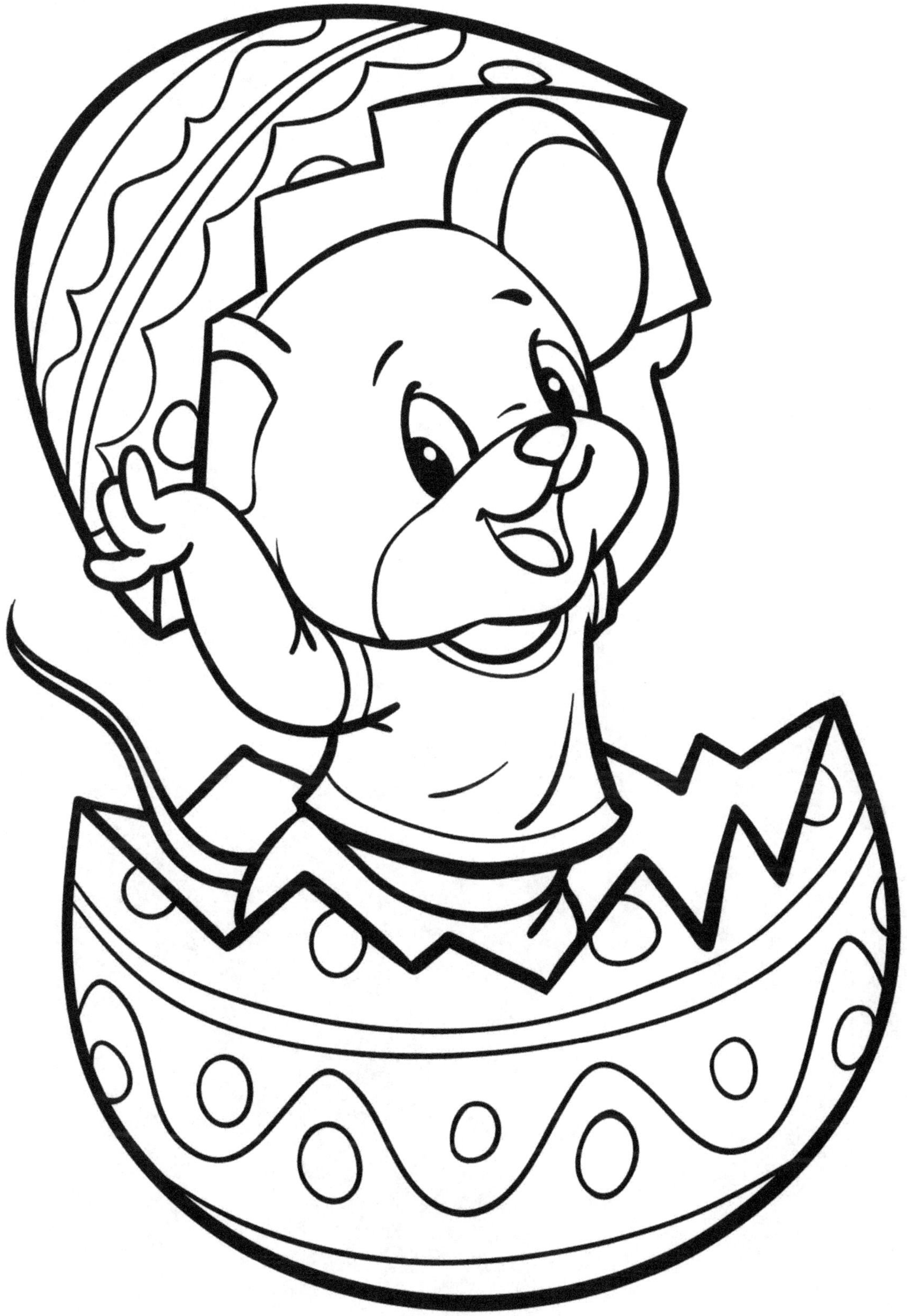

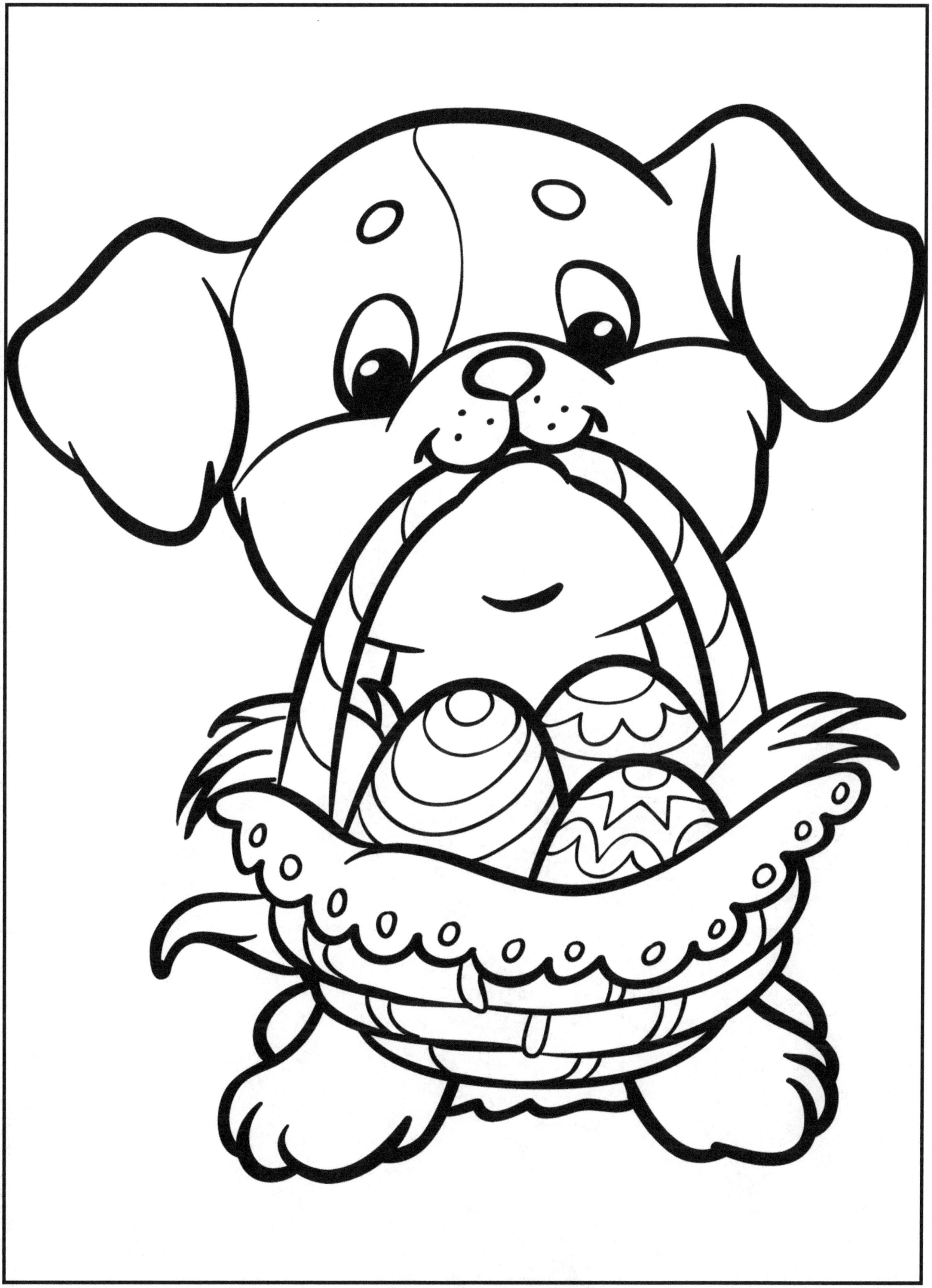

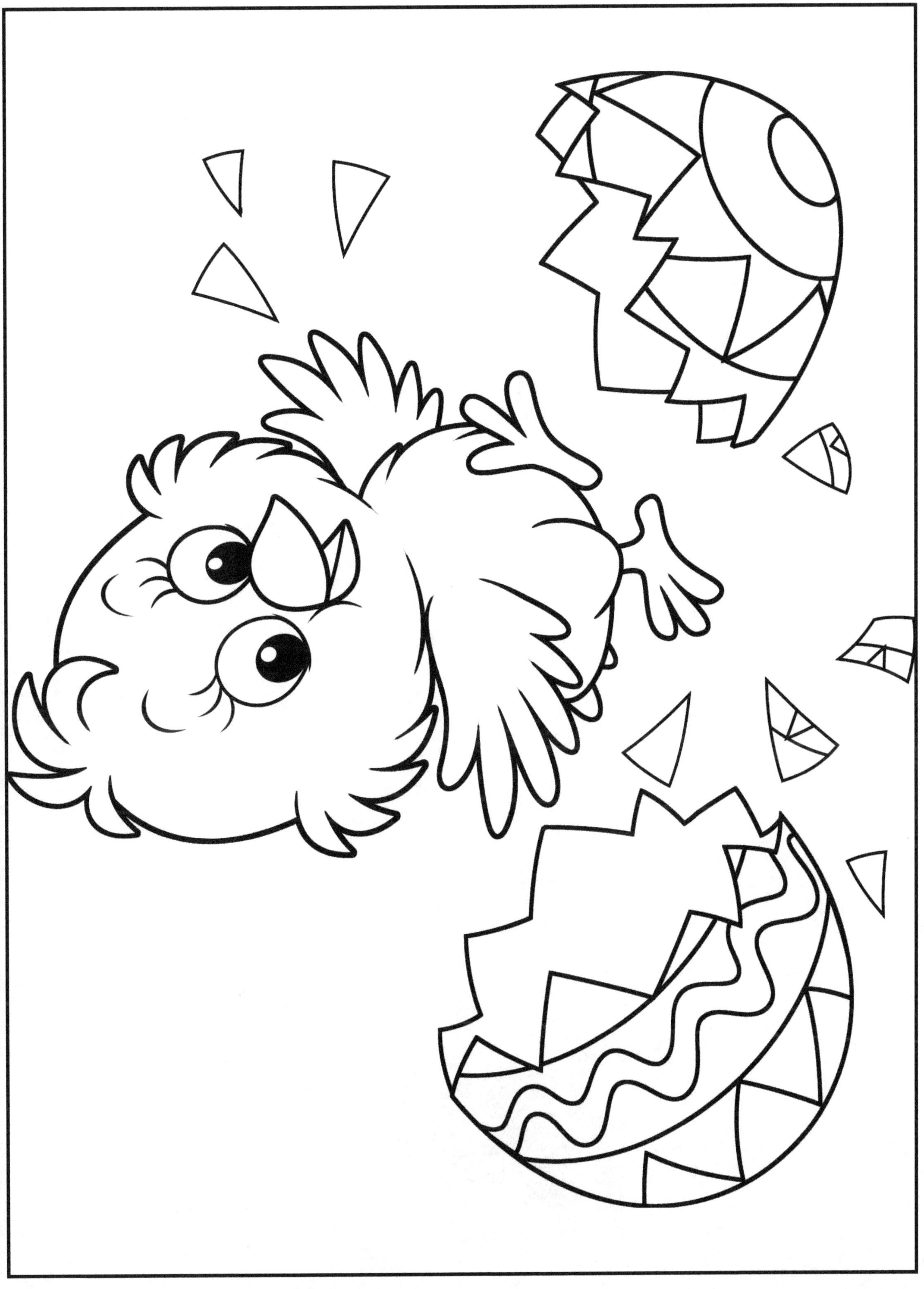

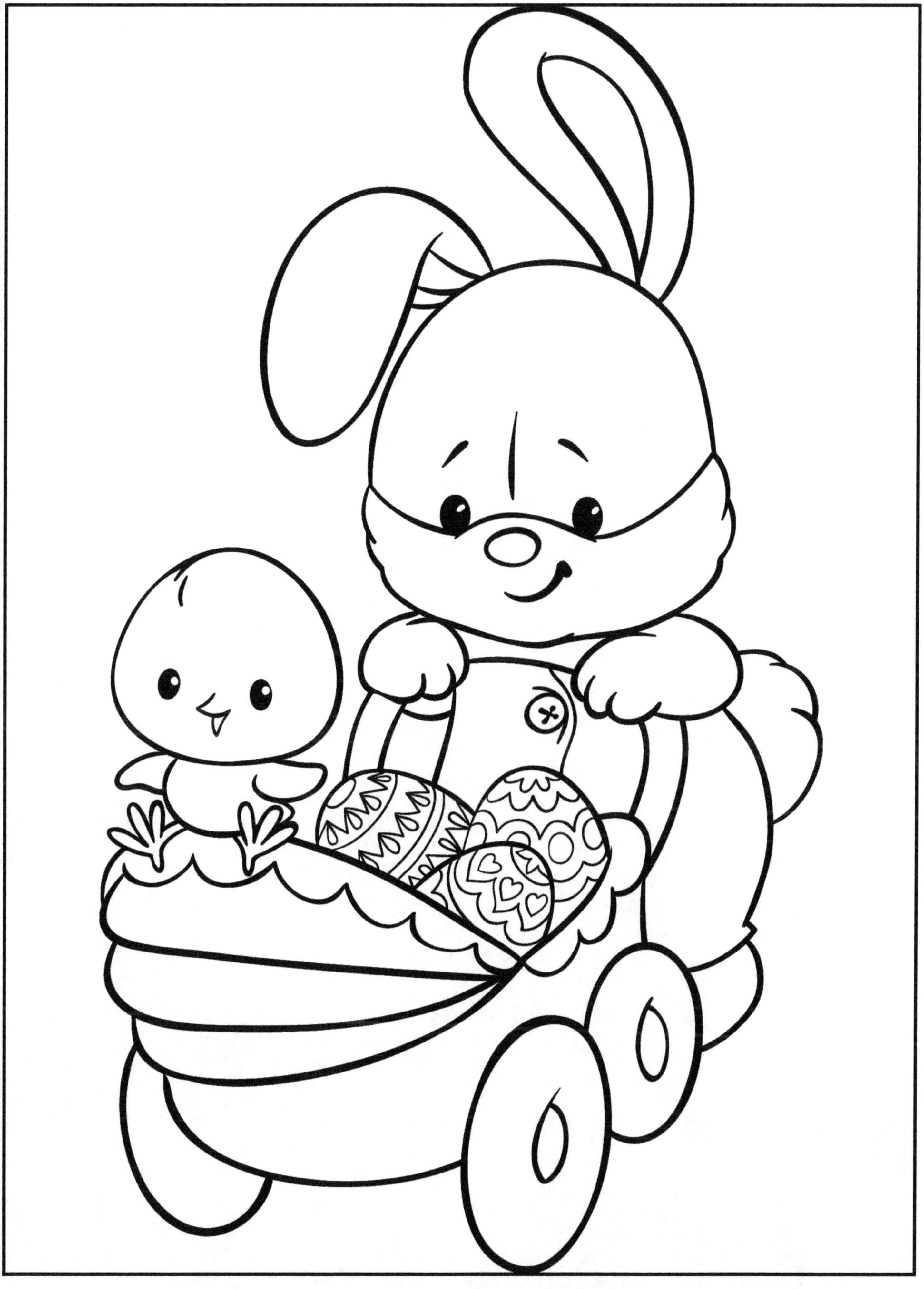

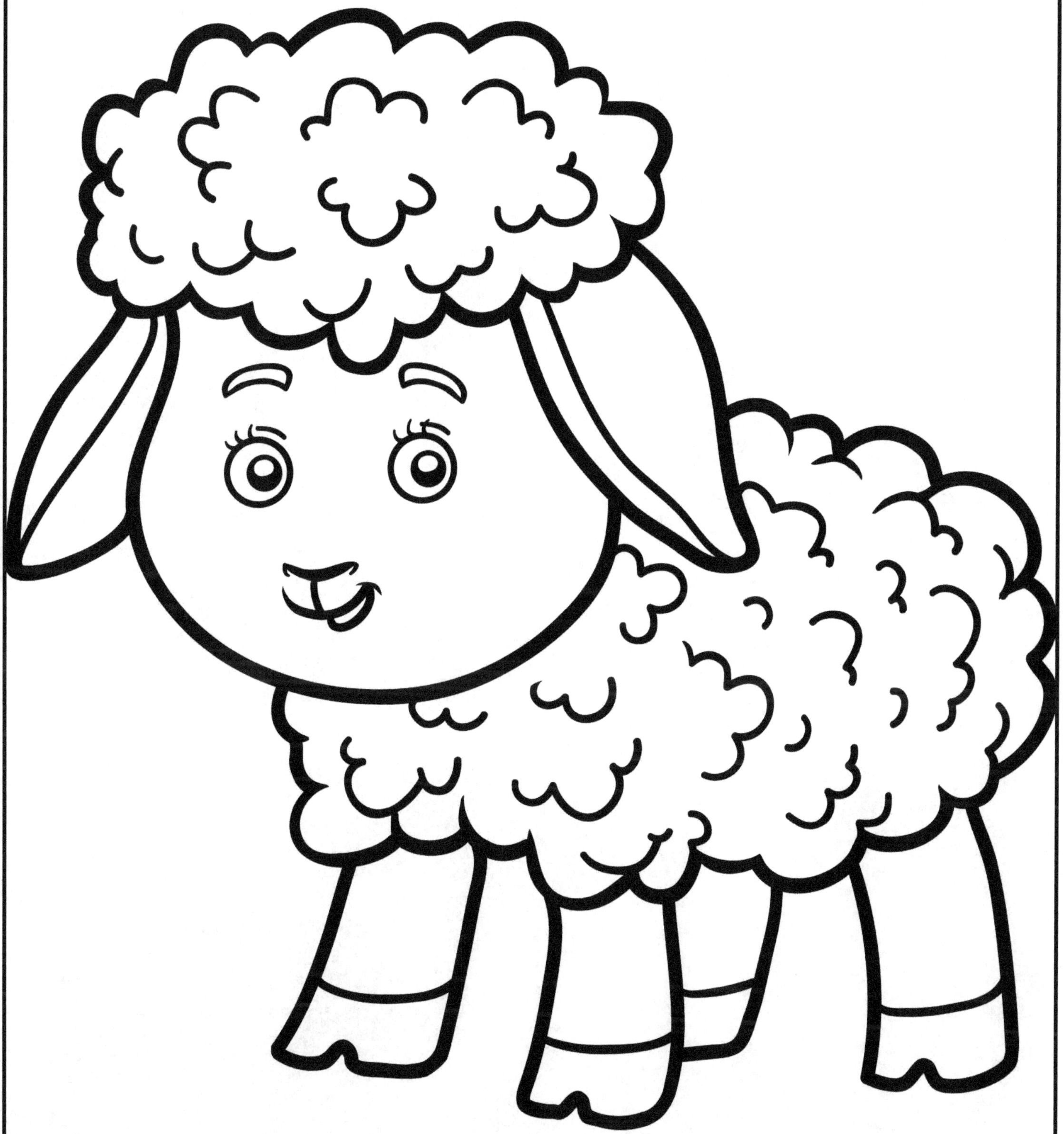

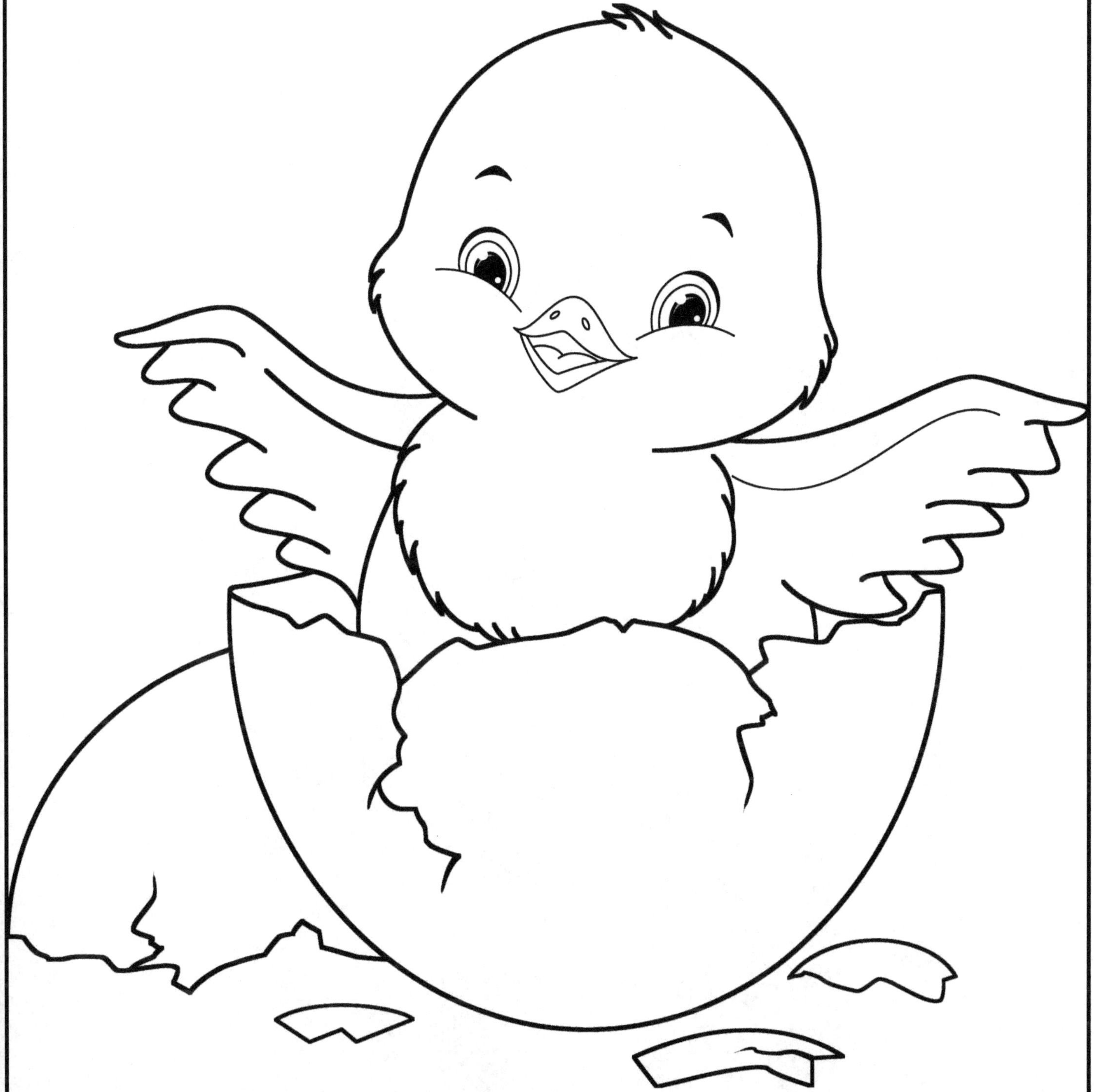

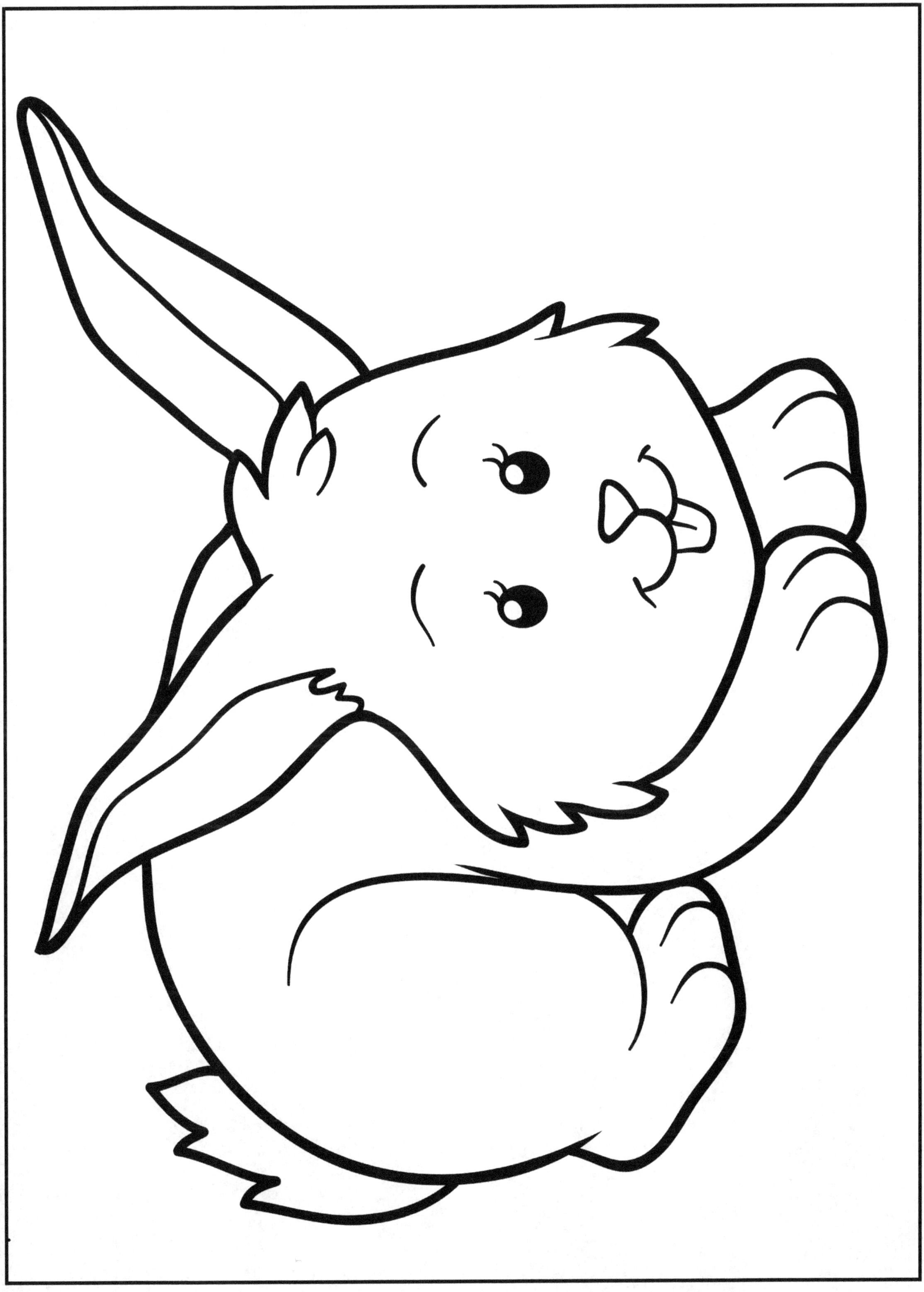

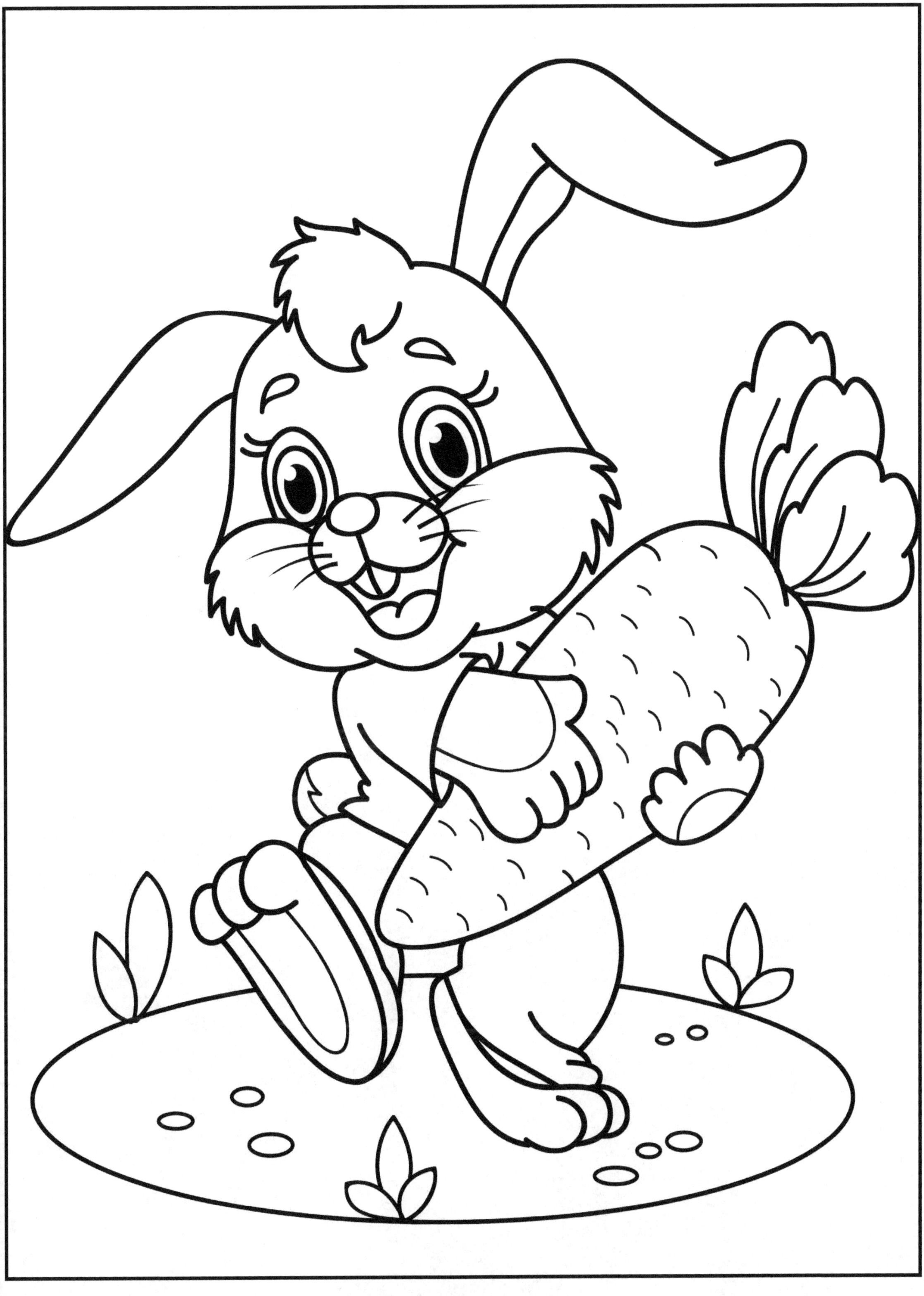

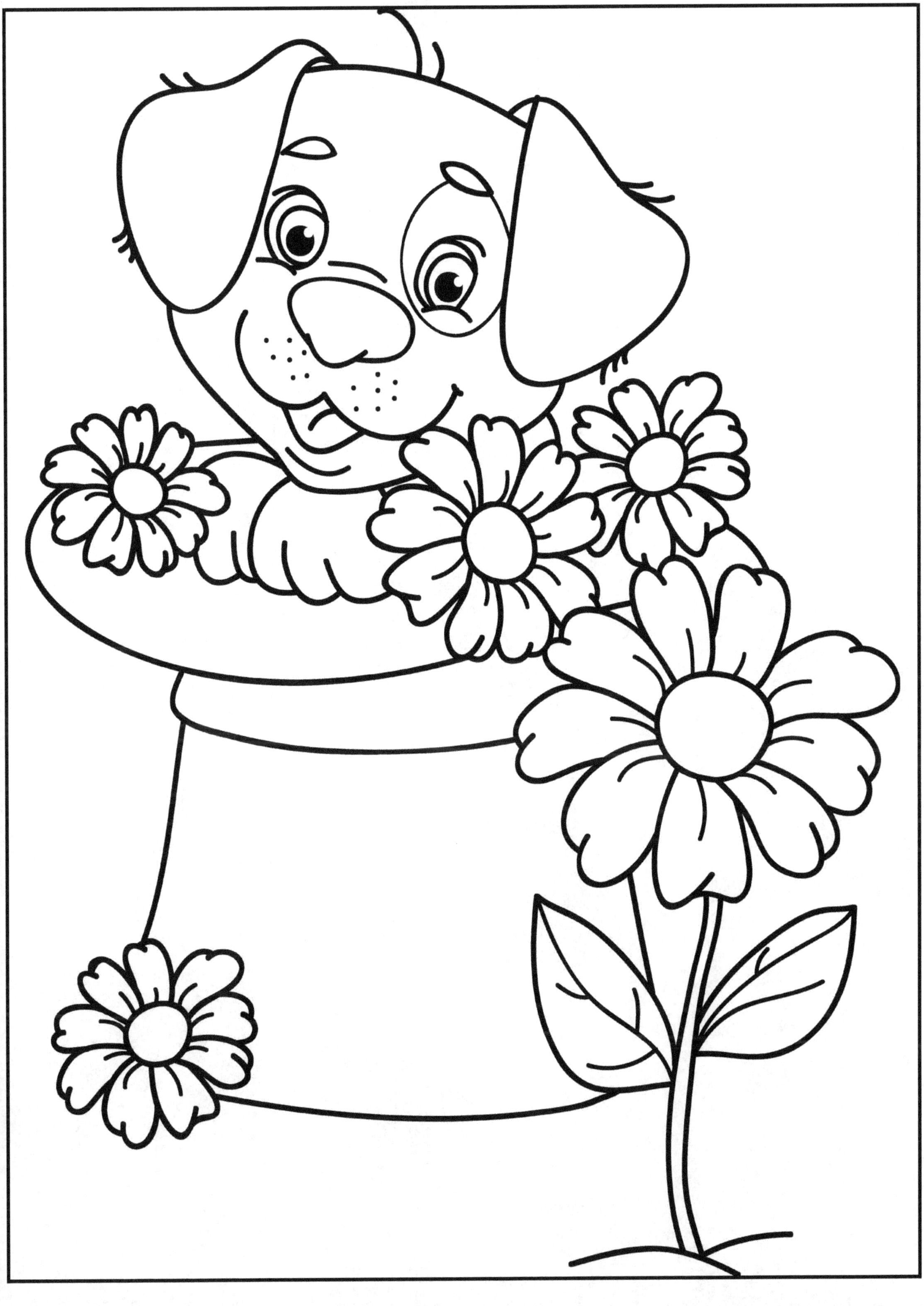

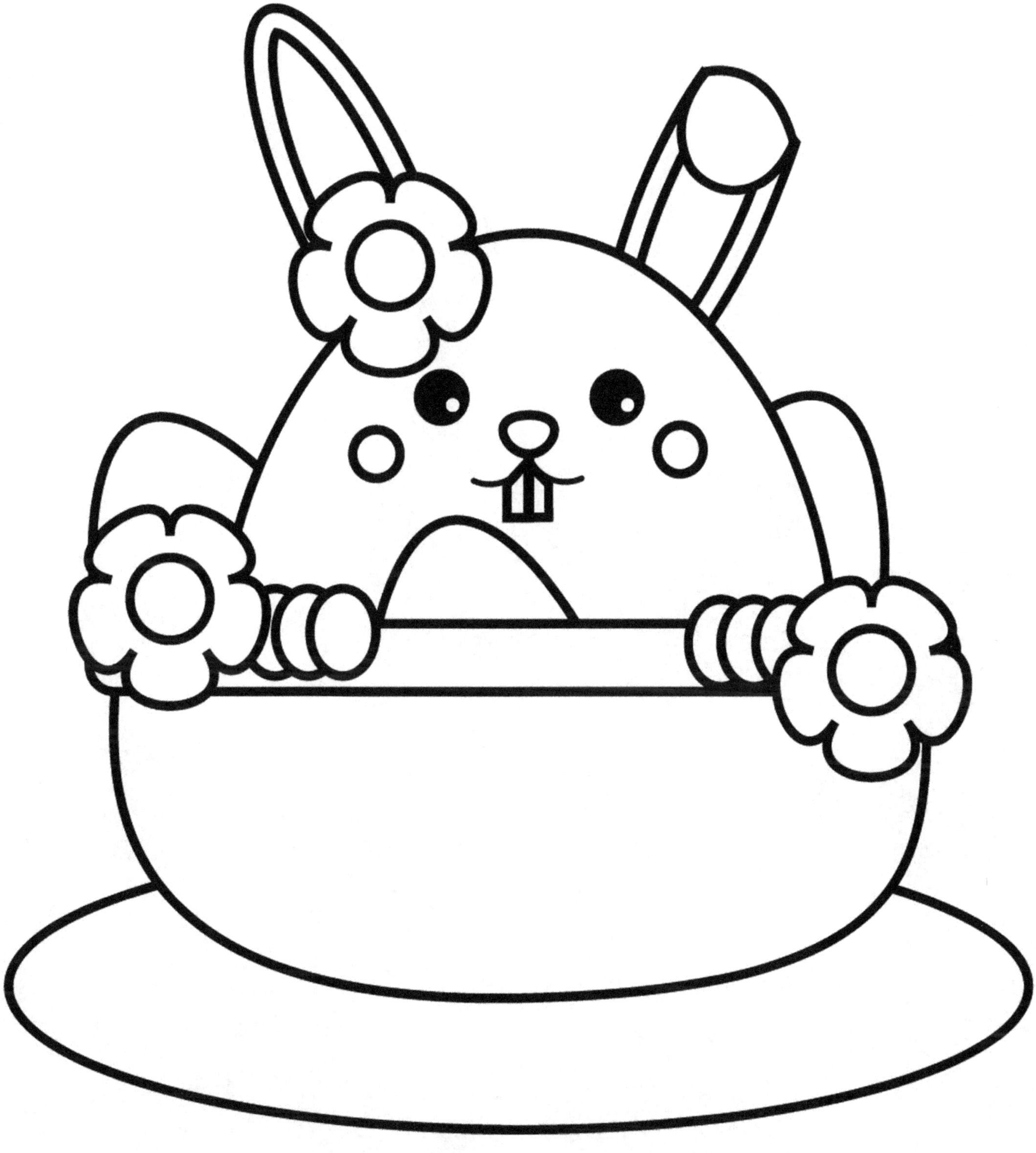

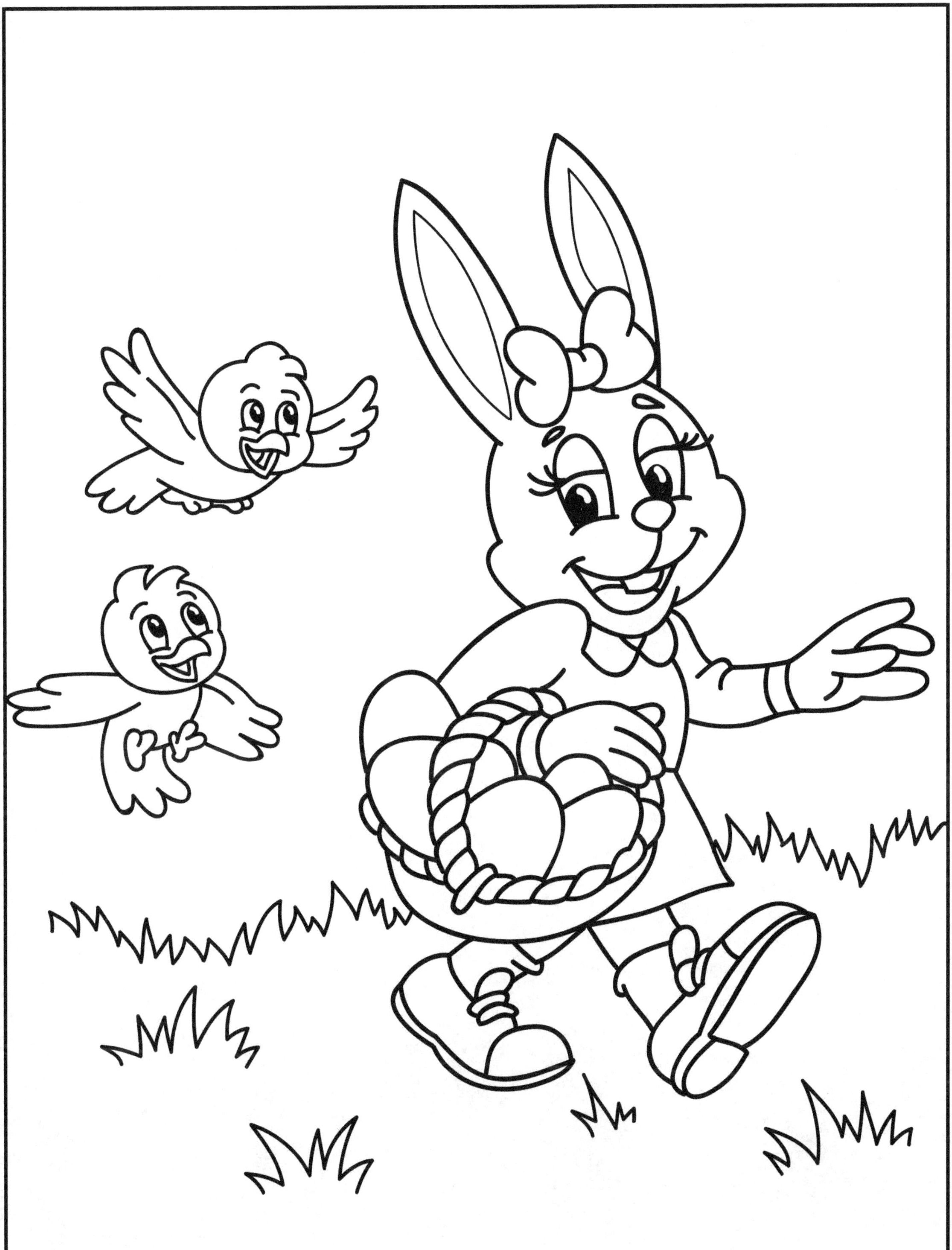

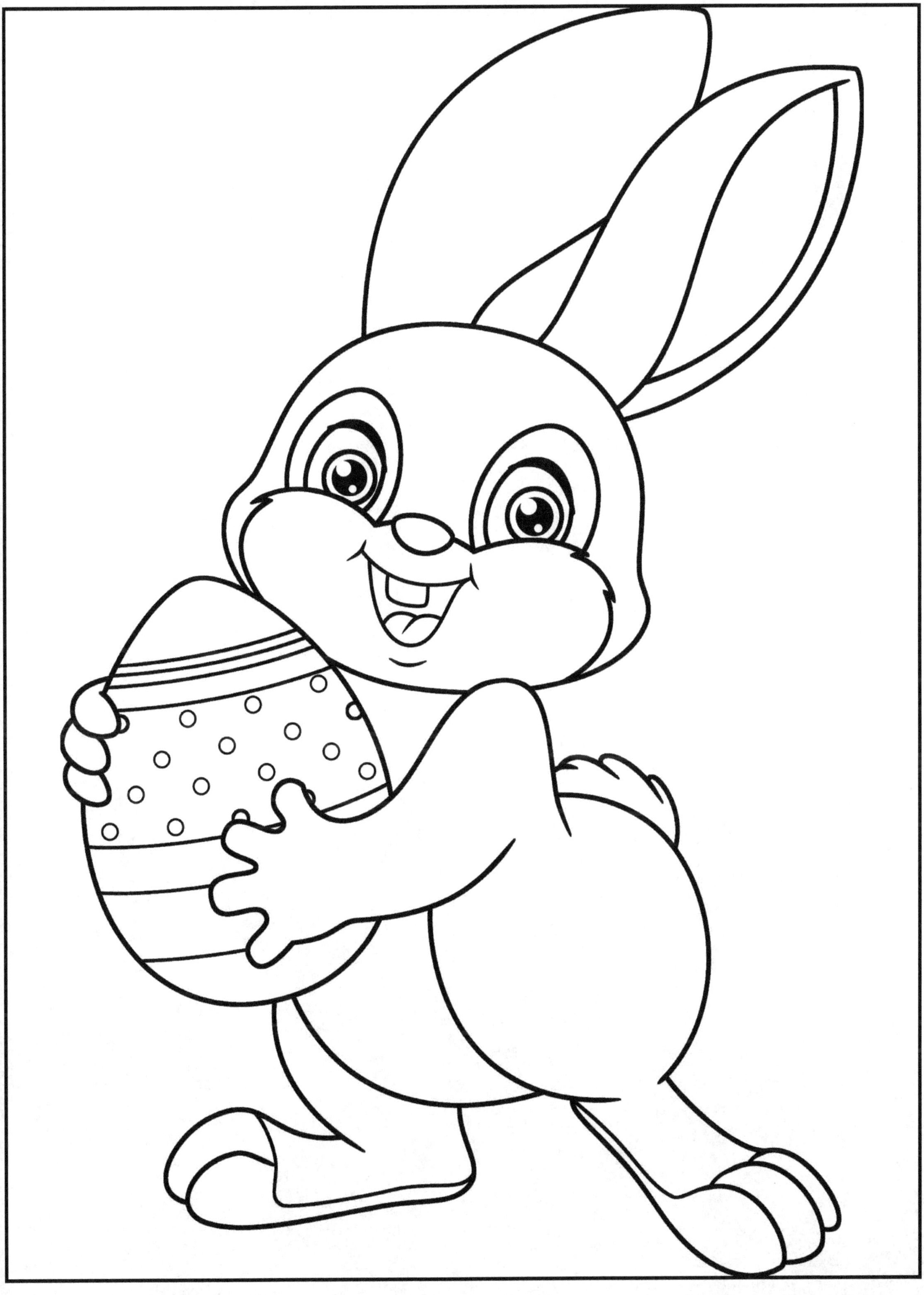

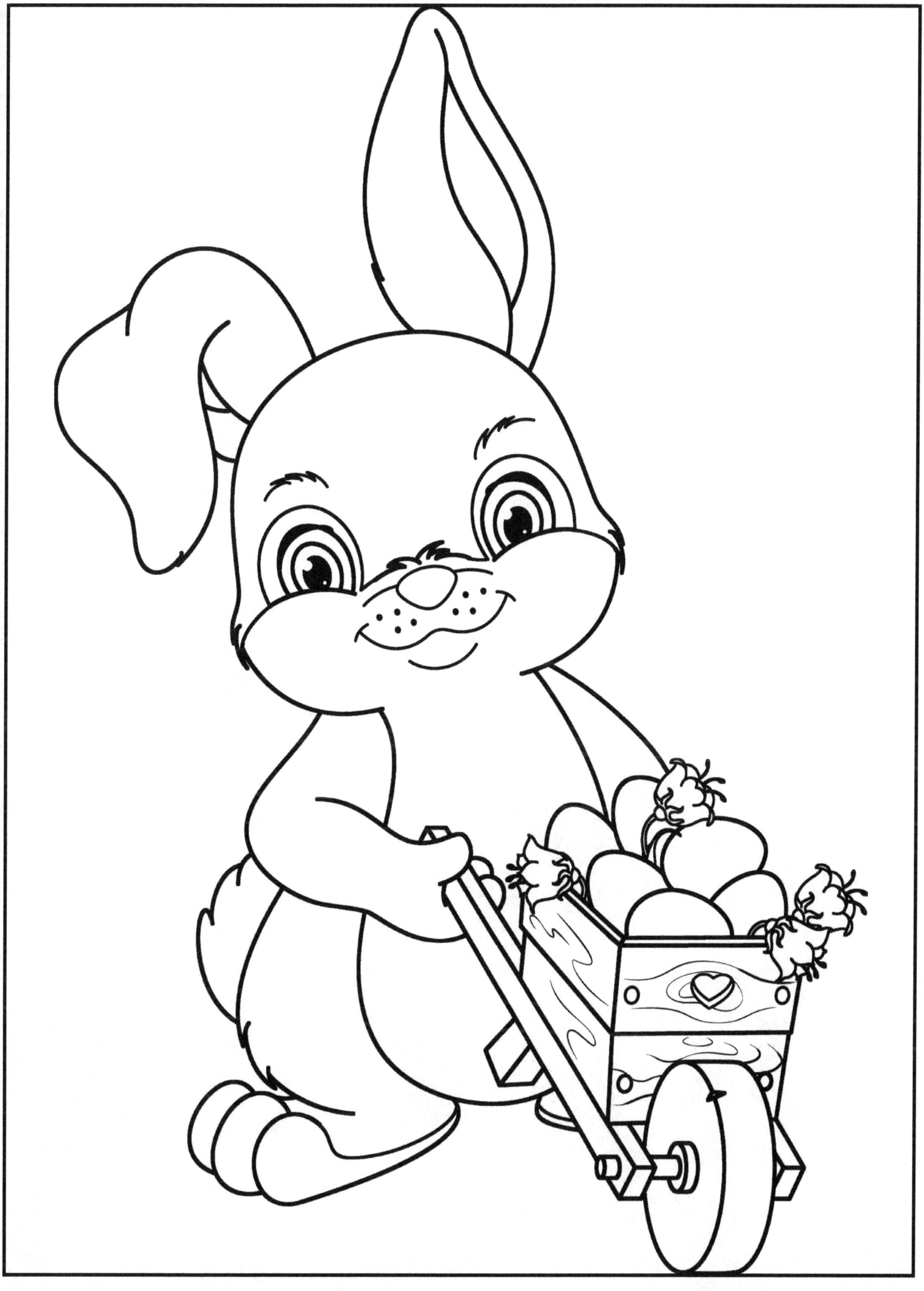

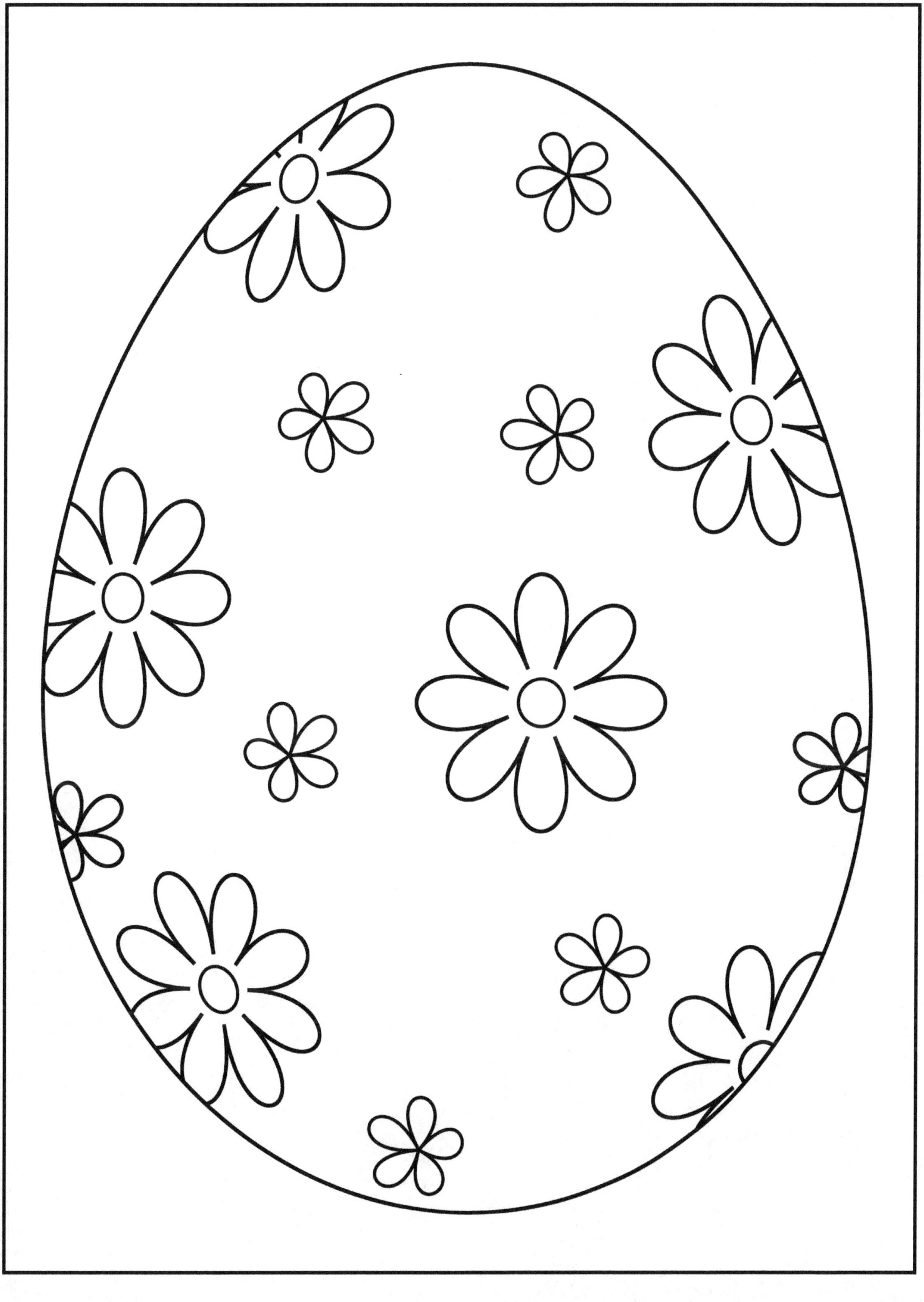

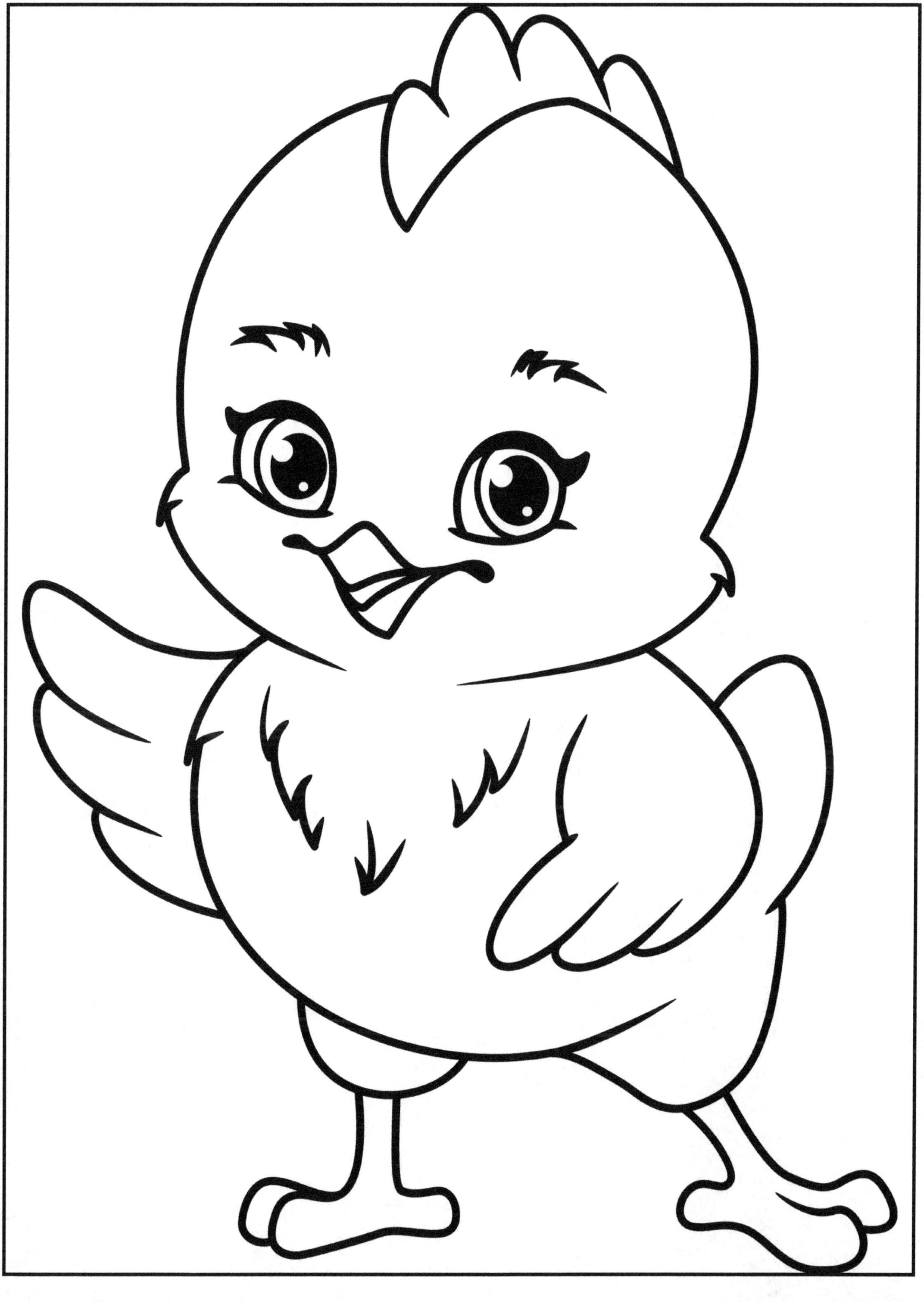

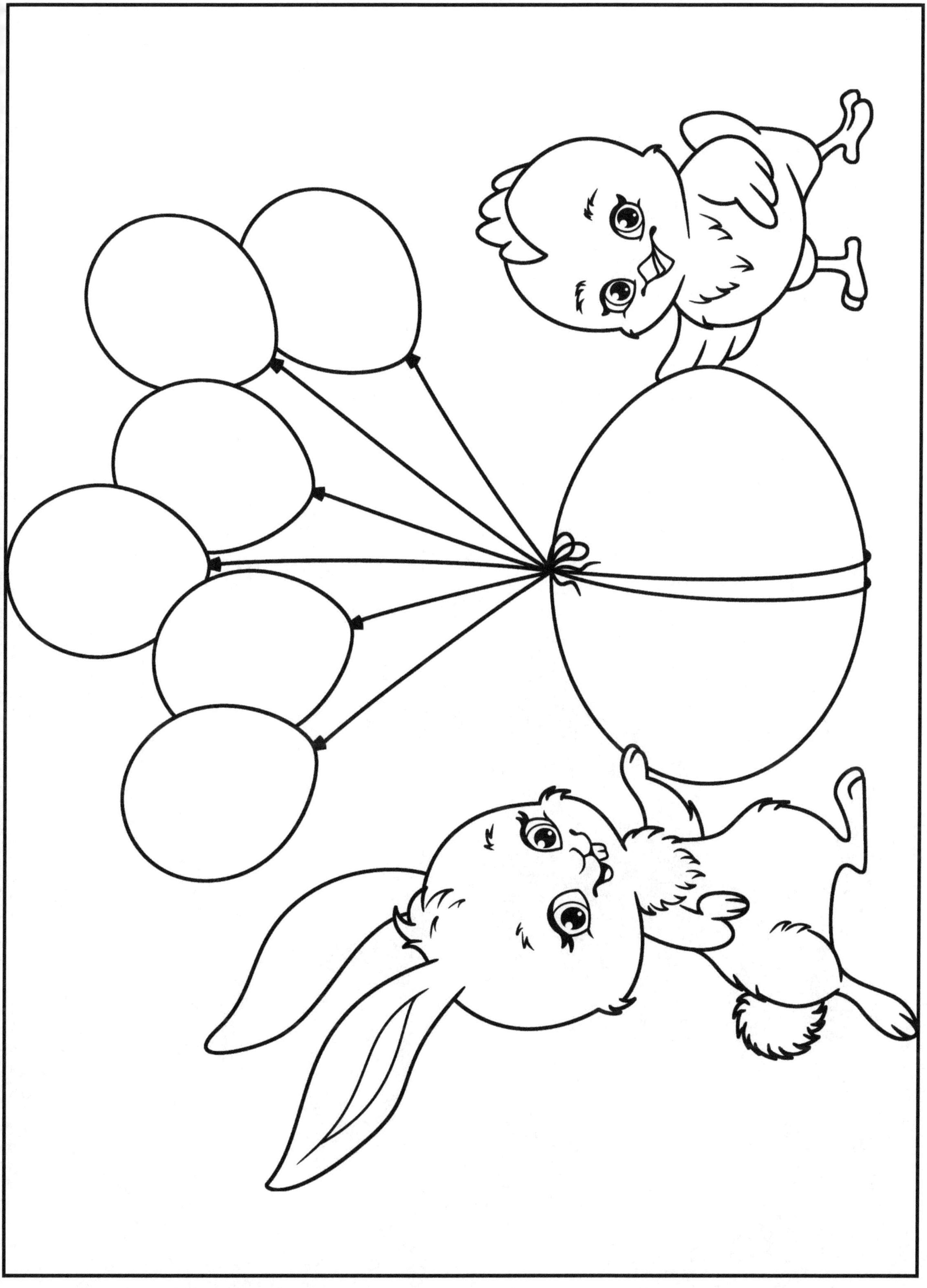

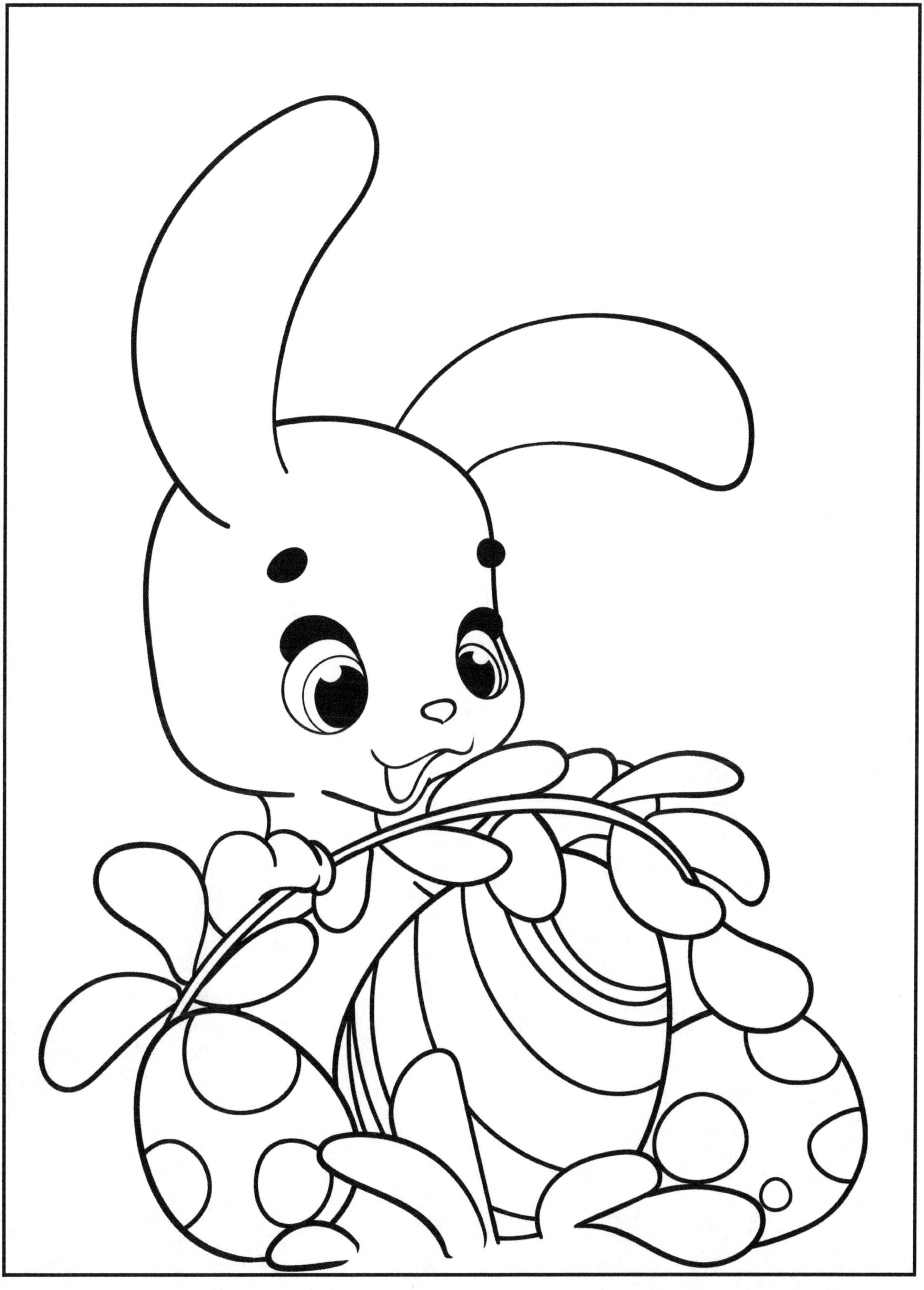

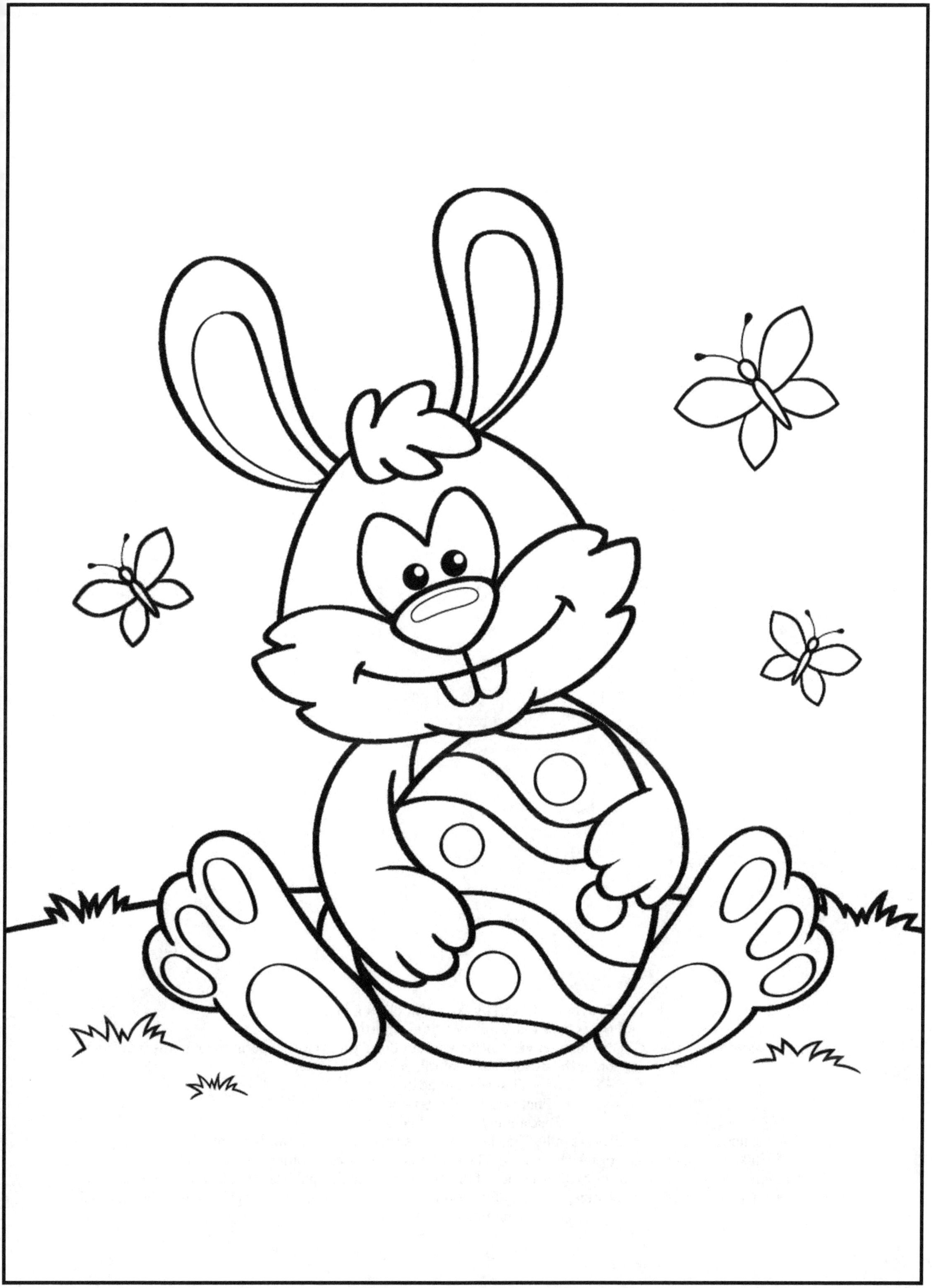

First edition: 2018
Photo credit: Shutterstock

9 781947 243668